MATHS

KEY STAGE TWO
SCOTTISH LEVELS C-E

SHAPE, SPACE AND MEASURES

JENNY NASH

Published by Scholastic Ltd,
Villiers House,
Clarendon Avenue,
Leamington Spa,
Warwickshire CV32 5PR
Text © Jenny Nash
© 1996 Scholastic Ltd
234567890   789012345

AUTHOR
JENNY NASH

EDITOR
MARGARET SHEPHERD

ASSISTANT EDITOR
LIBBY WEAVER

SERIES DESIGNER
LYNNE JOESBURY

DESIGNER
ANNA OLIWA

ILLUSTRATIONS
SALLY ROBSON

COVER ILLUSTRATION
JONATHAN BENTLEY

INFORMATION TECHNOLOGY CONSULTANT
MARTIN BLOWS

SCOTTISH 5–14 LINKS
MARGARET SCOTT AND SUSAN GOW

Designed using Aldus Pagemaker
Printed in Great Britain by Ebenezer Baylis
Worcester

British Library Cataloguing-in-Publication Data
A catalogue record for this book is available from the
British Library.

ISBN 0-590-53394-0

Contents

SHAPE, SPACE
AND MEASURES

Introduction

Scholastic Curriculum Bank is a series for all primary teachers, providing an essential planning tool for devising comprehensive schemes of work as well as an easily accessible and varied bank of practical, classroom-tested activities with photocopiable resources.

Designed to help planning for and implementation of progression, differentiation and assessment, *Scholastic Curriculum Bank* offers a structured range of stimulating activities with clearly stated learning objectives that reflect the programmes of study, and detailed lesson plans that allow busy teachers to put ideas into practice with the minimum amount of preparation time. The photocopiable sheets that accompany many of the activities provide ways of integrating knowledge and skills, differentiation, assessment and record-keeping.

Opportunities for assessment are highlighted within the activities where appropriate. Ways of using information technology for different purposes and in different contexts, as a tool for communicating and handling information and as a means of investigating, are integrated into the activities where appropriate and more explicit guidance is provided at the end of the book.

The series covers all the primary curriculum subjects, with separate books for Key Stages 1 and 2 or Scottish Levels A–B and C–E. It can be used as a flexible resource with any scheme, to fulfil National Curriculum and Scottish 5–14 requirements and to provide children with a variety of different learning experiences that will lead to effective acquisition of skills and knowledge.

SCHOLASTIC CURRICULUM BANK MATHEMATICS

The *Scholastic Curriculum Bank Mathematics* books enable teachers to plan comprehensive and structured coverage of the mathematics curriculum and pupils to develop the required skills, knowledge and understanding through activities that promote mathematical thinking and ways of working.

There are two books for Key Stage 1 / Scottish Levels A–B and two for Key Stage 2 / Scottish Levels C–E reflecting the sections of the programmes of study:
▲ Number (including Handling Data);
▲ Shape, Space and Measures.

Using and Applying Mathematics is integrated into these contexts as required by the National Curriculum and these links are highlighted on the grid on pages 156 and 157.

Bank of activities

This book provides a bank of activities that can be used in many different ways – to form a framework for a scheme of work; to provide breadth, variety or extension to a core scheme; to supplement a mathematical or cross-curricular topic; or they can be set as tasks to answer specific, individual learning requirements.

Range

The range of activities provided will enable pupils to develop mathematical language. They will need to select and use a variety of materials, and they will have appropriate contexts for measuring and using IT.

Communication skills

The activities aim to develop mathematical language and communication skills by encouraging children to:
▲ use mathematical vocabulary, diagrams and symbols;
▲ describe and discuss their work, and respond to questioning;
▲ present their work using a variety of mathematical forms;
▲ use and apply mathematics in everyday situations and within mathematics itself.

Lesson plans

Detailed lesson plans, under clear headings, are given for each activity and are set out in a standard way so that the material is easy to follow and can be readily implemented in the classroom. The structure for each activity is as follows:

Activity title box

The information contained in the title box at the beginning of each activity outlines the following key aspects:
▲ *Activity title and learning objective.* Each activity has a clearly stated learning objective given in bold italics. These learning objectives break down aspects of the programmes of study into manageable teaching and learning chunks, and their purpose is to aid planning for progression. These objectives can be easily referenced to the National Curriculum and Scottish 5–14 requirements by using the overview grids at the end of this chapter.
▲ *Class organisation/Likely duration.* Icons ✝✝ and ◷ signpost the suggested group sizes for each activity and the approximate amount of time required to complete it. Small groups will generally mean up to four to six children whereas larger groups could be ten to twelve children, or half the class. Timing arrangements are by their very nature arbitrary as so many factors are involved. Sometimes teachers may wish to extend the time spent on practical work and discussion and at other times children may find the task easier or harder than expected, which will in turn affect the time taken to complete it.

Previous skills/knowledge needed

The information given here alerts teachers to particular knowledge or skills that pupils need prior to carrying out the activity.

Key background information

The information given in this section is intended to set the scene and provide helpful guidance for teachers. The guidance may relate to pupils' learning, teachers' knowledge of mathematics or both.

Preparation

Advice is given for those occasions where it is necessary to orientate the pupils to the activity or to collect and prepare materials ahead of time.

Resources needed

All the equipment, materials and photocopiable sheets needed to carry out the activity are listed here, so that the pupils or teacher can gather them together easily before beginning the teaching session.

What to do

Easy-to-follow, step-by-step instructions are given for carrying out the activity, including, where appropriate, suggestions for suitable points for discussion. Issues of classroom management are raised where relevant.

Suggestion(s) for extension/support

Where possible, ways of modifying or extending tasks, for easy differentiation are suggested. Thus the activities are accessible both to less able and more able pupils.

Assessment opportunities

Each activity has clearly stated assessment opportunities which relate directly to the learning objectives for that activity

SHAPE, SPACE AND MEASURES

and provide the framework for ongoing assessment. By taking advantage of these assessment opportunities teachers can reassure themselves that the stated learning objectives have been achieved. Where appropriate, teachers' questions for eliciting information from pupils are also included.

Opportunities for IT
Where opportunities for IT present themselves, these are outlined briefly with reference to particularly suitable types of program. The chart on page 159 presents specific areas of IT covered in the activities, together with more detailed support on how to apply particular types of program. Selected lesson plans serve as models for other activities by providing more comprehensive guidance on the application of IT, and these are indicated by the bold page numbers on the grid and the ◈ icon at the start of an activity.

Display ideas
In this section any ideas for displays in the classroom and the maths corner are incorporated into the lesson plans.

Reference to photocopiable sheets
Where activities include photocopiable sheets, small facsimiles of the relevant sheets are included in the lesson plans, with notes describing how they can be used.

Summative assessment
There will be key points where teachers wish to take an overview of each pupil's achievement in mathematics. The final chapter contains assessment activities which enable teachers to address a number of the learning objectives contained within each chapter of the book. Assessment activities are indicated by the ◈ icon.

Using and applying mathematics
Aspects of using and applying mathematics are integral to each activity. Using and applying mathematics cannot be taught separately from the other areas of mathematics. It must be set in the context of mathematical content. It should be thought of more as a teaching approach and a mathematical process than as a distinct and separate content area and relies strongly on the ability to challenge pupils through questioning and extending tasks to follow alternative suggestions to support the development of reasoning. Therefore, on pages 156 and 157 a grid relating each activity to using and applying mathematics is provided. This grid will enable teachers to ensure that sufficient time and attention is paid to this central area of mathematics.

Photocopiable sheets
Many of the activities are accompanied by photocopiable sheets. For some activities, there may be more than one version; a sheet may be 'generic' with a facility for the teacher

to choose the appropriate task in order to provide differentiation by task. Other sheets may be more open-ended to provide differentiation by outcome. The photocopiable sheets are ideal for assessment and can be kept as records in pupils' portfolios of work.

Cross-curricular links
Cross-curricular links are identified on a simple grid (on page 160) which cross-references particular areas of study in mathematics to the programmes of study for other subjects.

SHAPE, SPACE AND MEASURES AT KEY STAGE 2

Young children spend much time exploring the three-dimensional space in which they live. They learn about shapes: how they pack and how they feel. They learn about the space in which they move and they learn how to make different sorts of movements. This informal understanding eventually develops so that they can make the classification of shapes that forms the beginnings of geometry along with the description of position and movement.

The ability to visualise shapes and movements supports the development of geometric ideas by giving children opportunities to make their own images based upon knowledge gained through practical activity. They learn to imagine shapes and movements, predicting and describing properties and changes before they physically see them. Such activity can help children learn to communicate their mathematics to others because it relies upon an ability to describe what is happening in their heads.

If descriptions are made using a common vocabulary others can share in the mathematical conversation and the need for convoluted descriptions is avoided; there comes a point when it is more efficient to identify a hexagon by its name than to launch into a list of the shape's properties. But in order to know what is meant by the word 'hexagon' the child needs to understand and remember its properties. So to study shape and space is to work on a set of related areas with a number of common features: the use of relevant mathematical language, the identification of properties and the description of movement.

The best teaching of measurement is also based on comprehensive practical work. Children acquire the language to describe their experience by discussing their activities. They begin to gain this language through the comparison and ordering of objects and quantities such as pencils, ribbons and stones. There is no need to use numbers at this stage but as children progress they learn to measure using non-standard units and then standard units which are counted. Measurement moves from being a comparison of objects and quantities with each other to become a comparison made with established units of measurement.

SHAPE, SPACE AND MEASURES

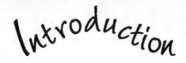

It thus becomes a process through which many number concepts such as more, less and fewer, addition, multiplication and subtraction as difference can be gained. As children progress, the areas of number and measures become more closely entwined along with the geometrical concepts involved in measuring angle, capacity and area. The estimation of length, mass, area, and volume also has much in common with aspects of mental geometry in that it requires children to form a mental image, this time of a given quantity against which the object being estimated is compared.

The need for standard units is based upon the requirement that measurement should be accurate enough for different people to make comparisons. As with shape and space, in order for different people to make comparisons they must all be speaking the same language, using and understanding a shared vocabulary.

All measurement is approximate and inexact. We can only ever measure a continuous quantity to a given degree of accuracy which in turn depends upon the purpose of the measuring as well as the accuracy of the instruments used. The Programme of Study for Shape, Space and Measures states that children working at Key Stage 2 should have opportunities to work in a variety of contexts. They should have experience of using geometrical properties and relationships to solve problems, extend their practical experience using a broad range of materials; use computers to transform shapes, work with a wide range of patterns, including those drawn from other cultural traditions; apply their measuring skills in a range of meaningful contexts.

Teachers need to ensure that children work on activities designed to help them learn about:

Three-dimensional shape
▲ To visualise and describe shapes and movements, using geometrical language to describe shapes;
▲ To make three-dimensional shapes and patterns accurately;
▲ To recognise the geometrical features and properties of shapes, classifying shapes and solving problems using these properties;
▲ The congruence of simple shapes;
▲ The reflective symmetries of three-dimensional shapes.

Two-dimensional shape
▲ To visualise and describe shapes and movements, using geometrical language to describe shapes;
▲ To make two-dimensional shapes and patterns accurately;
▲ To recognise the geometrical features and properties of two-dimensional shapes, classifying shapes and solving problems using these properties;
▲ The congruence of simple shapes;
▲ The reflective and rotational symmetries of two-dimensional shapes.

Position and movement
▲ To use reflection, rotation and translation to transform shapes;
▲ To visualise movements and simple transformations in order to create and describe patterns;
▲ To use coordinates to specify location;
▲ To use angles – right angles, fractions of a turn, degrees – to measure rotation using the associated language of angle.

Length
▲ To choose appropriate standard units of length, making sensible estimates with them in everyday situations;
▲ To develop understanding of relationships between units;
▲ To convert one metric unit to another;
▲ To know rough metric equivalents of Imperial units in use;
▲ To find perimeters of simple shapes, using practical methods to find the circumferences of circles including the introduction of the ratio ;
▲ To choose and use appropriate instruments for measuring length, to interpret numbers and read scales increasingly accurately.

Area
▲ To find areas by counting methods, leading to the use of other practical methods such as dissecting shapes.

Mass
▲ To choose appropriate standard units of mass, making sensible estimates with them in everyday situations;
▲ To develop understanding of relationships between units;
▲ To convert from one metric unit to another;
▲ To know rough metric equivalents of Imperial units in use;
▲ To choose and use appropriate instruments for measuring mass, interpreting numbers and reading scales increasingly accurately.

Capacity and volume
▲ To choose appropriate standard units of capacity, making sensible estimates with them in everyday situations;
▲ To develop understanding of relationships between units;
▲ To convert from one metric unit to another;
▲ To know rough metric equivalents of Imperial units in use;
▲ To choose and use appropriate instruments for measuring capacity and volume, interpreting numbers and reading scales increasingly accurately;
▲ To find volumes by counting cubes.

Time
▲ To choose appropriate standard units of time, making sensible estimates with them in everyday situations;
▲ To develop understanding of relationships between units;
▲ To choose and use appropriate instruments for measuring time, interpreting numbers and reading scales increasingly accurately.

SHAPE, SPACE
AND MEASURES

Learning objective	PoS/AO	Content	Type of activity	Page
Three-dimensional shape				
To revise the names of the more common three-dimensional shapes and to describe them using appropriate language. To visualise three-dimensional shapes.	2a, c. *Range of shapes: Level C.*	Describing three-dimensional shapes using correct mathematical terminology. Remembering position. Visualising three-dimensional shapes.	Small groups. Playing a memory game in which shapes are removed from a collection and children have to identify and describe those that have been removed.	14
To explore, visualise and construct cubes. To develop mental images of cubes and describe them.	2a, b. *Range of shapes: Level D.*	Working with imagery, cubes and nets.	Group and individuals. Discussing properties. Working on mental images of cubes. Unfolding cubes. Investigating nets of cubes. Recording.	15
To explore and construct prisms. To visualise and describe prisms using appropriate language.	2b. *Range of shapes: Level E.*	Properties of prisms. Construction of prisms using and applying knowledge of properties. Visualising and describing prisms.	Group, pairs and individuals. Identifying difference between a pyramid and a prism through discussion. Learning properties of prisms. Constructing a net of a given prism.	17
To sort three-dimensional shapes according to their properties. To use mathematical terminology to describe the features of three-dimensional shapes.	2a. *Range of shapes: Level D.*	Describing three-dimensional shapes using correct mathematical terminology. Sorting and classifying.	Group then individuals. · Completing Venn diagrams by sorting shapes into correct regions. Identifying the rule for sorting. Recording.	19
To explore the reflective symmetries of three-dimensional shapes.	2c. *Range of shapes: Level D. Symmetry: Level D.*	Defining planes of symmetry. Identifying planes of symmetry. Constructing three-dimensional shapes with planes of symmetry.	Group and individuals. Making models of simple three-dimensional shapes and cutting to show symmetries. Making models with a given number of planes of symmetry.	21
To construct nets for irregular three-dimensional shapes. To use isometric paper to represent three-dimensional shapes.	2a, b. *Range of shapes: Level D.*	Working with imagery, representing three-dimensional shapes in two dimensions. Constructing nets.	Individuals. Using isometric paper to represent models made with four cubes. Choosing models to construct nets.	23
Two-dimensional shape				
To make irregular shapes by folding. To visualise two-dimensional shapes.	2a, b. *Range of shapes: Level D.*	Terminology of two-dimensional shape. Recognising irregular polygons. Introducing heptagons and nonagons. Presenting results.	Individuals. Investigating folding rectangles to make shapes with different numbers of sides. Extending to square, triangles and hexagons. Recording.	26
To visualise, describe and name two-dimensional shapes. To create different polygons by cutting a square. To use the properties of shapes during investigation.	2a, b. *Range of shapes: Level D.*	Visualising shapes. Recognising and naming shapes. Describing their properties.	Individuals. Investigating making two cuts on squares to create shapes. Recording.	27
To introduce the idea of congruence of simple shapes. To identify congruent shapes.	2c. *Range of shapes: Level D.*	Introducing congruence. Identifying congruent regular and irregular polygons.	Group, pairs and individuals. Finding congruent shapes in a feely bag. Identifying congruent pairs of polygons on photocopiable sheet.	28

SHAPE, SPACE
AND MEASURES

Learning objective	PoS/AO	Content	Type of activity	Page
To identify equilateral, isosceles and scalene triangles and know their properties.	2a. *Range of shapes: Level D.*	Recognising, describing and naming equilateral, isosceles and scalene triangles.	Individuals. Making triangles with geostrips. Joining corners on shapes, searching for different types of triangles in regions created.	30
To identify the rotational and reflective symmetries of common regular quadrilaterals.	2c. *Symmetry: Level E.*	Symmetry properties of rectangles, squares, rhombuses, trapeziums, parallelograms.	Group and individuals. Testing polygons for symmetry using mirrors or by folding. Identifying orders of rotational symmetry by drawing around shapes and rotation. Recording.	31
To investigate patterns made by drawing successively smaller two-dimensional shapes.	2a, b. *Range of shapes: Level D.*	Constructing patterns accurately using two-dimensional shapes.	Individuals. Drawing shapes, measuring sides and using measurements to construct patterns.	33
Position and movement				
To use rotation to create patterns. To visualise movements and develop the use of mathematical language to describe patterns.	3a. *Shape, position and movement: Level E.*	Turning through 90°, 180°, 270°. Using rotation in visualising and making patterns.	Individuals and pairs. Designing and making tiles. Using them to construct patterns by rotation. Recording the patterns. Devising instructions to enable patterns to be reconstructed.	36
To construct two-dimensional shapes with reflective symmetry. To recognise reflective symmetry in irregular and regular shapes.	2c; 3a. *Symmetry: Level C.*	Sorting shapes according to symmetry. Identifying symmetry. Using knowledge and understanding of symmetry.	Individuals. Using three shapes to construct shapes with symmetry. Recording solutions.	37
To complete unfinished reflections of shapes. To use mirrors to create shapes. To use geometrical relationships to solve problems.	3a. *Symmetry: Level C.*	Completing part-drawn reflections of shapes using mirrors.	Individuals. Experimenting with mirrors to make new shapes. Completing reflections. Using a mirror on a shape to copy given shapes. Recording.	39
To use reflection and translation to create patterns. To analyse and describe patterns in terms of the transformations used to make them. To consider patterns from other cultural traditions.	3a. *Shape, position and movement: Level D.*	Flipping shapes vertically and horizontally and sliding them to make patterns.	Individuals. Analysing patterns and describing how reflection and translation have been used. Making patterns by reflecting and translating triangles. Recording.	41
To use degrees to measure rotation. To develop accuracy in making and estimating angles. To use protractors to measure angles.	3c. *Angle: Level D.*	Rotating strips to make angles. Measuring angles. Estimating angles.	Pairs. A game involving estimating, creating and measuring given angles to a given degree of accuracy.	42
To use coordinates to specify two-dimensional shapes. To transform shapes by translation on a grid.	3b. *Shape, position and movement: Level D.*	Plotting coordinates of two-dimensional shapes. Transforming shapes on a grid by translation.	Individuals working within a group. Plotting and recording coordinates of squares, rectangles and triangles. Exploring ways to translate shapes by adding or subtracting constants. Recording.	43

SHAPE, SPACE
AND MEASURES

Learning objective	PoS/AO	Content	Type of activity	Page
Length				
To estimate and measure using centimetres. To use measuring instruments. To develop a visual model of some lengths to use when estimating and measuring.	4a, b. *Measure and estimate: Level B.*	Exploring lengths using coloured rods.	Group and pairs. Estimating and measuring. Recording.	46
To use and apply knowledge of measuring length to solve problems. To use measuring instruments to measure in centimetres.	4a, b. *Measure: Level B.*	Making a length of paper one metre long.	Pairs. Using one piece of paper to make a metre strip. Measuring in centimetres.	47
To find perimeters. To make shapes with a given perimeter.	4a, c. *Measure: Level C.*	Establishing meaning of perimeter. Making shapes with different perimeters from pattern blocks.	Individuals. Measuring perimeters using centimetres, deciding which blocks to use. Recording.	49
To estimate and measure using millimetres. To translate between centimetres and millimetres.	4a, b. *Measure and estimate: Level D.*	Measuring small objects that fit into a matchbox.	Small groups and individuals. Finding a number of objects to fit into a matchbox. Measuring them using millimetres. Translating between millimetres and centimetres. Recording.	52
To use metric and Imperial measures. To know the rough metric equivalents of Imperial units.	4a, b. *Measure: Level D.*	Measuring body parts using feet and inches. Learning the rough metric equivalents of Imperial units of length.	Small groups. Labelling pictures with measurements. Recording.	53
Area				
To find areas by counting squares. To investigate shapes with constant areas.	4c. *Measure: Level C.*	Finding areas of squares and rectangles by counting squares.	Large group and individuals. Investigating area of squares on geoboards. Investigating rectangles with constant areas. Recording.	56
To find areas by counting squares, including part squares. To estimate and approximate areas.	4c. *Measure: Level C.*	Finding areas of irregular shapes. Counting parts of squares.	Large group and individuals. Investigating methods of finding areas of irregular shapes. Recording.	58
To compare shapes with equal areas but different perimeters.	4c. *Measure: Level C.*	Finding shapes with constant areas and differing perimeters.	Individuals. Recording.	59
To find areas of shapes by methods involving dissection.	4c. *Measure: Level C.*	Finding areas of quadrilaterals by rearranging shapes to form rectangles.	Small groups and individuals. Dissecting shapes and finding areas. Recording.	61
Mass				
To estimate and measure in grams.	4a, b. *Measure and estimate: Level C.*	Estimating the order by mass of a number of objects. Checking by measuring.	Pairs. Finding the mass of objects using balances. Recording.	64
To estimate and find in grams and kilograms. To convert between metric units of mass. To interpret scales on measuring instruments.	4a, b. *Measure and estimate: Level C.*	Estimating and measuring in grams. Converting between grams and kilograms.	Pairs. Finding the combined mass of three potatoes using measuring instruments. Recording as grams and as kilograms and grams.	66

SHAPE, SPACE AND MEASURES

Learning objective	PoS/AO	Content	Type of activity	Page
To calculate using standard units. To solve problems involving mass. To interpret measuring instruments.	4a. *Number, Money, Measure: Level D.*	Calculating the cost of portions of food. Gross and net weights. Comparing packages for value for money.	Individuals or pairs. Investigating value for money. Recording.	68
To use metric and Imperial units. To know the approximate metric equivalents of Imperial units.	4a, b. *Measure: Level D.*	Finding the mass of filled bags using measuring instruments. Measuring in Imperial units. Rough metric equivalents of pounds and ounces.	Small groups. Finding the mass of bags filled with different amounts. Recording.	70
Capacity and volume				
To use 100ml units when measuring capacity. To make and use measuring instruments to estimate the capacity of containers to the nearest 100ml. To read and interpret scales on measuring instruments.	4a, b. *Measure: Level D.*	Making a calibrated measuring container. Estimating and measuring the capacity of containers.	Small groups and pairs. Use of measuring instruments. Recording.	74
To make reasonable estimates of the capacity of containers. To use measuring instruments to measure in litres and millilitres.	4a. *Measure and estimate: Level D.*	Estimating and measuring the capacity of containers in litres and millilitres.	Whole class and pairs. Estimation and measurement of capacity of containers. Recording.	75
To find volumes by counting cubes. To develop an understanding of the need for a formula for the volume of a cuboid $v = l \times b \times h$.	4c. *Measure: Level D.*	Building cubes and cuboids. Finding volumes.	Large group, pairs and individuals. Measuring volumes by counting cubes. Introduction of formula. Recording.	77
To know Imperial units of capacity and their approximate equivalents.	4a, b. *Measure: Level D.*	Comparing the capacity of containers. Relationship between pints and litres.	Large group and individuals. Use of different units of measurement.	79
Time				
To tell the time to the nearest minute. To use and interpret digital and analogue clocks and record times.	4a, b. *Time: Level C.*	Using digital and analogue clock-faces. Identifying the starting time of TV programmes and recording.	Groups, pairs and individuals. Recording times on digital and analogue clock-faces. Using TV guides.	82
To use stopwatches to time events to the nearest tenth and hundredth of a second. To read and interpret displays on stopwatches.	4a, b. *Time: Level C.*	Estimating and measuring time taken to carry out events.	Groups and pairs. Recording estimates and time taken.	84
To calculate with 12-hour times.	4a. *Time: Level D.*	Counting in five- and ten-minute intervals. Adding and subtracting times to calculate the length of programmes.	Individuals. Using TV guides. Recording.	85
To order events using 12-hour clock and 24-hour clock times and understand the relationship between the 12- and 24-hour systems.	4a. *Time: Level D.*	The convention of the 24-hour clock. Equivalent 12- and 24-hour times.	Large or small groups, then individuals. Children draw and illustrate a 24-hour time line. Recording.	87

Entries given in italics relate to the Scottish 5–14 Guidelines for Mathematics.

SHAPE, SPACE AND MEASURES

Three-dimensional shape

Children's understanding of three-dimensional shape develops from a number of activities used to further understanding of either two-dimensional shapes or position and movement. Children today are more comfortable than many adults when working with three-dimensional shapes because they have experience from their earliest school days in building with, sorting and classifying shapes. They can name common shapes and begin to use appropriate mathematical terminology to describe them.

Solid shapes, or polyhedra, have three-dimensions: length, width and height. In order to name a shape, children need to attach a set of attributes to it, for example a cube has six congruent square faces, eight vertices and twelve edges and is a member of the set of cuboids. This approach helps the children as they work with more complex polyhedra and ask themselves a series of questions so that they can identify particular shapes. Children need to use mathematical language and be able to sort and classify shapes. They need practice in looking at, discussing, visualising, taking apart commercial packages, making and constructing shapes. Discussion is important because it is through talking with children that the teacher can find out what they are thinking, how much they understand and how they view things.

Geometrical work should involve visualising shapes and there are strong links with using and applying mathematics. Children should be encouraged to anticipate how something will look before constructing it or picking it up.

13

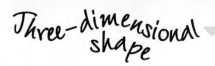

MEMORY GAME

To revise the names of the more common three-dimensional shapes and to describe them using appropriate language. To visualise three-dimensional shapes.

†† *Small groups.*

🕐 *20 minutes.*

Previous skills/knowledge needed

The children should have worked with three-dimensional shapes and be able to name some of them. They should be beginning to describe three-dimensional shapes in terms of their mathematical properties.

Key background information

The ability to memorise shapes and their positions is important both in everyday life and mathematics. If children can visualise a shape they have internalised its features but they may not yet be able to describe those features. This version of 'Kim's Game' is designed to help children to develop this expertise.

Preparation

Prepare a tray of three-dimensional shapes arranged in rows. These should be those shapes with which the children are familiar, and will probably include cubes, cuboids, spheres, cylinders, pyramids and cones. Older or more able children may work with prisms, different sorts of pyramids and more complex polyhedra with an increasing number of faces. Ensure that the names of the shapes are displayed somewhere in the classroom so that the children can refer

to them if necessary. Photocopy page 104 as a reference for each group.

Resources needed

A tray or large box lid, a cloth, three-dimensional shapes, rough paper, copies of photocopiable page 104.

What to do

Work with the whole group. Hold a brief discussion in which you revise the names of three-dimensional shapes with the aid of some examples. Then hold up a shape (a pyramid is a good one to choose), let the children look at it for about 20 seconds and then hide it. Ask them to tell you as much as they can about it, encouraging the children to concentrate on the mathematical properties. When they have remembered as much as they can, tell the children that they are going to be doing something similar but with more shapes so ask them to suggest any ideas that they have for helping memorise them. The idea of taking a photograph in their minds and then recalling it is often a popular one, but others may include concentrating on recalling one face at a time or recollecting different views.

Remove the cloth from the tray and let the children look at it for 20 seconds or so. Ask the children to hide their eyes while you remove one shape. When they open their eyes ask them to work out which shape has been removed and then ask questions to elicit discussion about the properties and name of the shape. How do they know? What was its position? What did it look like? Can they remember everything about the shape? It is important to show the children the shape in its original position when you have finished. Continue by removing different shapes. Eventually you could rearrange

SHAPE, SPACE AND MEASURES

Sorting three-dimensional shapes (2)

Name(s) _____ Date _____

Some useful words to use when describing three-dimensional shapes.

Face
Edge
Vertex
Vertices
Base
Regular
Equal
Flat
Curved
Straight
Right Angle
Equilateral
Square
Triangular
Circular
Rectangular
Hexagon
Pentagon
Prism

the shapes, placing them in random positions or remove more than one shape at a time. The photocopiable sheet can be used to help children make use of the appropriate vocabulary.

Suggestion(s) for extension

Rearrange the shapes or put some different ones on the tray. Give the children a little longer to look at the tray and then ask them to draw a quick sketch of the shapes in their correct positions. This is surprisingly difficult so the children could write the names of the shapes in the correct positions instead. They then compare their results in pairs and decide on a final version as a result of their discussion before checking by lifting the cloth.

Suggestion(s) for support

Use fewer shapes on the tray and lift the cloth for a longer period to let the children absorb the contents of the tray. You could have a duplicate set of shapes and ask the children to use them to work out which was missing from the tray.

Assessment opportunities

How proficient are the children at identifying the missing shapes? Are the children using the correct language to describe the three-dimensional shapes? Can they describe them using appropriate mathematical language and terminology? Can they name the shapes? Can they tell you the mathematical properties of the shapes? Can they recall and describe the positions of the shapes?

Reference to photocopiable sheet

Photocopiable page 104 offers the children a number of relevant mathematical terms to use when describing three-dimensional shapes.

CUBES

To explore, visualise and construct cubes. To develop mental images of cubes and describe them.

†† *Groups and individuals.*

⏰ *75 minutes (for both parts).*

Previous skills/knowledge needed

The children should have had experience of building with different three-dimensional shapes such as building bricks, construction kits and reclaimed materials. They should have some knowledge of cubes and other common three-dimensional shapes.

Key background information

A cube is a member of the set of cuboids. A cuboid is a solid shape which has six rectangular faces and opposite faces which are congruent. A cube has six rectangular faces which are square, eight vertices and twelve edges. An edge is the line where two faces meet. Two or more edges meet at a vertex (corner). The net of a cube is the plane (two-dimensional) shape which can be folded to make a cube. There are eleven different nets of a cube.

Preparation

Construct some cubes using Clixi or Polydron. Look at the 'What to do' section below and try out the mental imagery activities yourself before the lesson. Photocopy page 100 for each child.

For the extension activity: draw the net of a cube, colouring each face differently and then construct the cube. Make a copy of photocopiable page 101 for each child doing the extension activity.

Resources needed

Cubes of various sorts (from sets of polyhedra, bricks, boxes), large squared paper, scissors, glue, adhesive tape, colouring pencils, Clixi or Polydron, photocopiable pages 100 and 101 (for the extension activity).

What to do

First part

Give each child a cube. Clarify its properties through discussion and practical activity by asking the children to run their fingers along an edge, point to a vertex, count the vertices, count the faces and edges and describe the faces. Ask them to change cubes with another child and check that the new cube has the same properties.

Now ask the children to close or cover their eyes. Work on mental imagery. Ask them to imagine a blue cube sitting on a table and use or choose from the following prompts: Colour the top of your cube red and the base yellow. How many faces are blue now? Turn the cube so that the red face is now the base. Turn it so that it is sitting on a blue face. What colour is the top now? Where is the yellow face? (Expect different answers to this one depending on which blue face they have made the base.) Describe your cube. Turn your cube so that the top is red and the base is yellow again. Run your finger around all the edges that touch the yellow face. How many are there? Imagine that you have cut the cube in half. What shapes are the halves? Can you cut it in half differently?

This is demanding, particularly if the children have not tackled similar activities, so work slowly. Stop at key points and encourage the children to talk about what they can see. It is a good idea to keep cubes on the table so that the children can look at them from time to time to help them construct their own mental images but try not to make the children over-reliant on this as a strategy.

Second part

Use a cube-shaped box and ask the children to imagine what it would look like if you cut it open. Indicate the edge that you would cut along. Ask for a number of solutions before cutting along the edge that you have indicated. Open up the box and look at how it is made with the group. Were their predictions correct? Are there any other ways to cut open the box? Will the net look the same if the box is cut differently? After discussion use the cube made from interlocking squares to try out two more ways of opening it up to form a net. Elicit the fact that each net is made of six squares and that they join along complete edges.

Introduce photocopiable page 100 and explain it to the children. Tell them that you want them to try to find all the possible nets of a cube. It is important that they draw as many possible nets before constructing the cubes as this encourages the children to visualise and predict, but as they progress to make the cubes they will probably find more nets. They should use the sheet to record their plans first and then test them by using Clixi or Polydron. They should mark their nets with a tick or cross. When they have finished the testing process, ask the children to compare results with the rest of their group and make a poster to show all the nets. Encourage the children to think about the similarities between those arrangements that will

fold up to make a cube and the similarities between those that will not fold up to make a cube.

Suggestion(s) for extension

Ask the children to use squared paper or card to construct cubes from their nets but make sure that these are large enough for the children to be able to join the edges easily. It is more challenging to draw the nets on plain card as the children have to measure and draw accurately. If a flap is drawn on every other edge as on photocopiable page 101 the joins will work quite well.

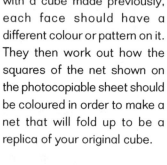

Use photocopiable page 101 to extend the children's use of mental imagery in working with cubes. Provide the group with a cube made previously, each face should have a different colour or pattern on it. They then work out how the squares of the net shown on the photocopiable sheet should be coloured in order to make a net that will fold up to be a replica of your original cube.

Suggestion(s) for support

Do not use photocopiable page 100. The children should work with Clixi or Polydron to find as many nets as possible by making a cube and then opening it in different ways. Each time they discover a new net they can record it on squared paper. Help them to recognise that rotations or reflections of a net are identical by encouraging them to turn their nets around.

Assessment opportunities

Talk to the children as they work on the mental part of the activity. Can they visualise a cube? How do they cope with rotating the cube? Can they tell you how the faces would be arranged if its orientation is changed? Can they 'count' the edges and vertices? Can they predict how a cube will look when it is opened up and flattened to form a net? Can they tell you any other ways of unfolding the cube? Are they able to predict how the net will look if the cube is unfolded in this way?

Examine the children's work on photocopiable page 100 and question them if necessary. Can they visualise the nets of cubes? Do they produce a large number of arrangements of squares that will not fold to make a cube? Can they explain why these do not 'work'? Can they draw nets of a cube?

Opportunities for IT

The children could use a drawing package to plan out their net for the cubes. It is usually possible to 'turn on' a background grid of squares which can be set at 1cm intervals. The children can use the grid to draw lengths of specific sizes. If the package has a *snap to grid* facility this will help the children to line up the sides of the cubes accurately and at 90°. Once the children have mastered the method of drawing lines they will find it easy to create a whole series of nets which can later be printed out and tested.

Display ideas

Much of the work produced will make an effective display, including the posters and any cubes made from nets. Display these along with other cubes (both environmental and from mathematical sets) to help the children make connections with the application of mathematical ideas in everyday life.

Reference to photocopiable sheets

Photocopiable page 100 is used to record the children's nets of cubes which they subsequently test out. Photocopiable page 101 is used for one of the extension activities; it provides the net of a cube for the children to decorate in order to fold up to make a replica of a given cube.

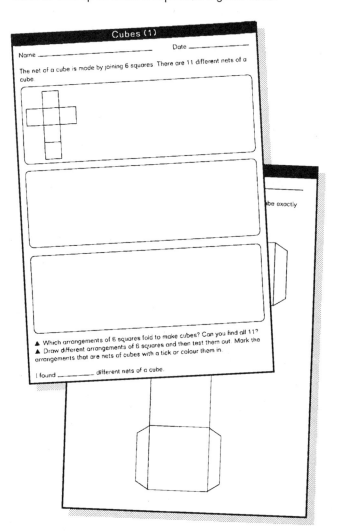

Cubes (1)

Name _____ Date _____

The net of a cube is made by joining 6 squares There are 11 different nets of a cube

▲ Which arrangements of 6 squares fold to make cubes? Can you find all 11?
▲ Draw different arrangements of 6 squares and then test them out. Mark the arrangements that are nets of cubes with a tick or colour them in.

I found _____ different nets of a cube.

PRISMS

To explore and construct prisms. To visualise and describe prisms using appropriate language.

†† Group, then pairs and individuals.

⏰ 60–75 minutes.

Previous skills/knowledge needed

The children should be familiar with common three-dimensional shapes. They should be able to describe their properties using appropriate mathematical language.

Key background information

A prism is a solid shape. Its end faces are congruent (identical in shape and size) and parallel. The cross-section formed by cutting the prism parallel to the end faces is congruent to the end faces. Most prisms are named after the shape of their end faces and the other faces of a prism are rectangular. Cuboids (and therefore cubes) are prisms.

Preparation

Revise the construction of nets with the group before you tackle this activity so that the children are able to tackle the net of a prism once they have learned its properties. Photocopy a few of photocopiable page 104 if you want to offer the children prompts to remind them of some mathematical terms. Photocopy a sufficient number of photocopiable page 102 to allow one copy for each pair of children.

Resources needed

Spheres, pyramids, cubes, cuboids, triangular prisms, a

SHAPE, SPACE AND MEASURES

number of other prisms (for example: pentagonal or hexagonal, these can include commercial packages such as chocolate boxes), thin card, scissors, rulers, glue, adhesive tape, photocopiable pages 104 and 106 (if required).

What to do

Show the group a tetrahedron and a triangular prism and ask the children to work in pairs for five minutes to list as many differences between the two shapes as possible. Ask them to concentrate on the mathematical properties of the shapes and to use the correct mathematical terms where they can. You might want to use photocopiable page 104 (prompt sheet from 'Sorting three-dimensional shapes') to help some children remember the mathematical terms that they should be using.

After five minutes use the children's lists as a basis for discussion and compile a whole group list in which all the differences are listed. This should include numbers of faces, edges and vertices, shape of faces, the fact that the tetrahedron has a 'point'. The children may notice that the faces of the tetrahedron are all congruent whereas the triangular pyramid has congruent end faces (triangles) and congruent rectangles. This discussion is valuable as it helps the children to 'practise' using mathematical language. It is important that you use the correct terminology whenever possible, giving alternative words as necessary for clarification but not replacing the mathematical words with everyday ones.

Go on to clarify the properties of a triangular prism with the children using the information in key background information if necessary. Ensure that the children are familiar with the terms 'congruent', 'parallel' and 'cross-section'. Then show them a hexagonal prism and elicit the similarities and differences between the two prisms. They should notice that the end faces of both polyhedra are joined by rectangles but

that the end faces are different shapes. Ask the children to explain why the hexagonal prism has more faces (because the end faces are hexagons and each edge of the hexagon is joined to a rectangle).

The children should now have worked sufficiently with prisms to know their properties and use these to decide whether a particular polyhedron is a prism or not. It is a good idea to offer them a cuboid at this point and ask them to consider whether it belongs to the set of prisms by going through these properties. Show the group some other prisms and other polyhedra to check their understanding.

Introduce photocopiable page 104 and explain the task. The children should make the net of the prism accurately. They will need to measure the edges of the faces carefully. If a flap is drawn on to every other edge, the prism can be folded up and stuck together.

Suggestion(s) for extension

The children can investigate the number of faces, edges and vertices for different prisms. They should draw a chart on which to record their findings. Encourage them to look for a relationship between the number of sides of the end face (for example, three on a triangle) and the total number of faces, edges and vertices. Can they explain the relationship? (The total number of faces is two more than the number of sides of an end face; the total number of edges is three times the number of sides on the end face; the total number of vertices is twice the number of sides on one of the end faces.)

Suggestion(s) for support

Once the initial discussion has been completed ask the children to make prisms using Clixi or Polydron. They can make cuboids, triangular prisms, hexagonal prisms and hexagonal prisms using the more common pieces. When

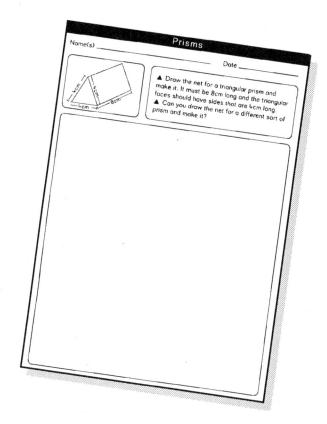

Reference to photocopiable sheets

Photocopiable page 104 provides a set of mathematical terms as a prompt for children as they identify the mathematical differences between the pyramids and prisms.

Photocopiable page 102 shows a triangular prism with measurements given and asks the children to make a net that folds to make a triangular prism with the same dimensions.

SORTING THREE-DIMENSIONAL SHAPES

To sort three-dimensional shapes according to their properties. To use mathematical terminology to describe the features of three-dimensional shapes.

†† *Group then individuals.*

⏱ *45 minutes.*

Previous skills/knowledge needed

The children should be able to recognise the properties of three-dimensional shapes and be able to use appropriate mathematical language to describe them. Their vocabulary should include faces, edges, vertices, curved, flat, congruent. Activities such as 'Memory game', 'Cubes' and 'Prisms' will help the children to develop the appropriate knowledge and understanding. They should be able to use and interpret Venn diagrams and tree diagrams.

Key background information

The identification of similarities and differences lies at the heart of much mathematical activity. In order to be able to name a shape a child has to be able to identify its attributes: the number of faces, their shapes, possibly the number of edges and vertices. Both cylinders and triangular prisms are members of the set of prisms but they look very different, so the process of asking oneself a series of questions based upon their mathematical properties has an important part to play in deciding how to classify them.

Preparation

Spend a few minutes revising the names of the solid shapes with the children. Encourage them to use the correct terminology to describe them. Photocopy page 103 for each child and make a few copies of photocopiable page 104 for reference within the group.

Resources needed

A set of three-dimensional shapes (cube, cuboid, square pyramid, tetrahedron, pentagonal pyramid, triangular prism, other prisms, cone, cylinder and sphere), other three-dimensional shapes (boxes, packages), photocopiable pages 103 and 104.

they have carried out this practical activity they can choose one of their prisms and open it, preferably along an edge joining two rectangular faces and then sketch the net. If preferred the net can be drawn using the same measurements on a large piece of paper or the children can make a scaled-down version of the net.

Assessment opportunities

How confident are the children at using the correct mathematical language to describe polyhedra? Can the children identify different prisms? Can they describe their properties? Can they identify all the faces, edges and vertices of prisms? Can they construct prisms from given nets? Can they construct prisms by drawing nets?

Opportunities for IT

The children could use a drawing package to draw a series of nets for making prisms. It is usually possible to 'turn on' a background grid of squares which can be set at 1cm intervals and used to help drawing lines of specific lengths. If the package has a *snap to grid* facility this will also help the children to line up the parts of the net.

Display ideas

Arrange a display of prisms. This should include commercial boxes, nets and children's models of different prisms. Display a list of the mathematical properties of prisms. If the display is kept for some time change the models daily and sometimes include polyhedra which are not prisms. The children can then identify the odd ones out.

SHAPE, SPACE AND MEASURES

What to do

Pass a shape around the group and ask each child to say something about it, for example: 'All the faces are square.' 'It's got eight edges.' 'The vertices are all right angles'. When the group has identified all the attributes of a shape, introduce a new one. Encourage the children to listen to each other's contributions, perhaps by asking individual children to tell you everything that has been said about a particular shape. This part of the activity will help the children to focus on the attributes of the shapes in order to prepare for the sorting and classifying aspects that follow. Introduce cubes, cuboids, cylinders, prisms and spheres.

Now choose a number of cubes and cuboids and ask the children to tell you what they all have in common. They may say that they have eight vertices, twelve edges, 24 right angles, six congruent faces, or all faces rectangular. Encourage all the children to identify as many attributes of the set as possible.

Draw a Venn diagram with an intersection, reminding the children that the intersection shows those shapes that have both attributes in common. Label the Venn diagram and ask each child in the group to take a shape if possible and put it on to the Venn diagram in the appropriate region. Ask them their reasons for placing a shape in a particular place. Other useful questions include: 'Could you put that cube in the intersection? Why not? Why doesn't it belong in this region?

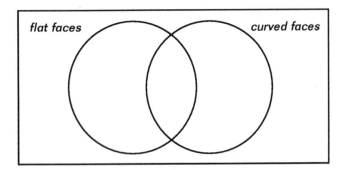

flat faces   curved faces

Now give each child a copy of photocopiable page 103. Clarify the task. They should sort shapes on to the Venn diagrams. The challenge to identify the criteria by which the shapes have been sorted in the final question is more demanding but is a useful method for assessing the depth of their understanding.

Suggestion(s) for extension

Ask the children to choose a set of four shapes. They then construct a tree diagram to identify each one. This can be made more challenging by asking them to work with more shapes. The most powerful question should be asked first so that the set is split into two equal parts as far as possible.

Suggestion(s) for support

Play a 'Twenty Questions' type game to encourage the children to look at shapes and become more familiar with their properties. A child or adult thinks of a shape and their partner has to work out which shape has been chosen by asking a question to which the answer can only be 'Yes' or 'No', for example: 'Does it have six faces? Are the faces all the same?' Encourage them to focus on mathematical attributes rather than colour or pattern if you are using commercial packs or coloured shapes from classroom sets.

If the children have trouble remembering the names of the shapes they could be labelled, as this will help them to associate the mathematical properties of shapes with their names. Photocopiable page 104 can be used as a prompt to help the children use the correct mathematical terminology.

Assessment opportunities

There will be opportunities to assess the children's understanding both as they work on the initial part of the activity and as they use the worksheet. If you are uncertain about the level of the children's understanding ask each one to choose three shapes and tell you as many ways as possible in which they are different. Can they use mathematical terminology appropriately? Do they use the correct words to describe three-dimensional shapes or do they use vocabulary that is more appropriate for describing two-dimensional shapes? Can they name the shapes?

Opportunities for IT

The children could use a branching database to create an electronic key for identifying the different three-dimensional shapes. This type of database differs from conventional ones in that the children must teach the software about the different shapes by phrasing questions that can only be answered with a yes or no. Answering *yes* to a question leads in one direction, *no* in another. This skill makes the task a good language activity as well. The resulting key can be used by other children to identify any object in the set of shapes.

For example asking the question:

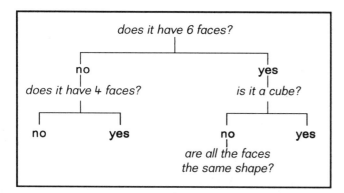

The activity is best organised in small groups with a limited range of shapes to begin with. A key part of the activity is to decide on the first question which will provide a good basis for splitting the whole set. Different groups of children can try out their database with other groups to test how easy it is to use and how accurate the answers are.

Reference to photocopiable sheets

Photocopiable page 103 provides Venn diagrams to be completed by the children. Children should write the names of the shapes in the appropriate part of each diagram. Some children may find it easier to draw the shapes.

Photocopiable page 104 provides a set of mathematical terms as a prompt for children working on the support activity. It could be used by other children as they work on the main activity.

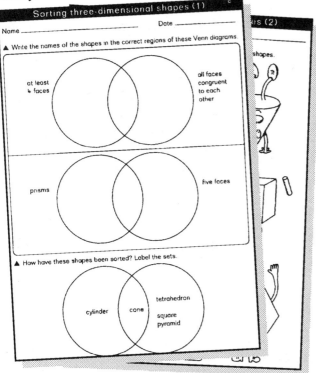

SYMMETRIES OF THREE-DIMENSIONAL SHAPES

To explore the reflective symmetries of three-dimensional shapes.

†† *Group and individuals.*

🕐 *30–40 minutes.*

Previous skills/knowledge needed

The children should be able to recognise the symmetries of two-dimensional shapes. They should have used mirrors to find or check lines of symmetry. They should know the mathematical properties of three-dimensional shapes.

Key background information

The mathematical features of three-dimensional shapes include their symmetries and as children become more confident mathematicians they are expected to add the symmetry properties of shapes to the others that they use to sort, classify and describe different polyhedra. Three-dimensional shapes have plane symmetry. A plane is a flat surface which can be vertical, horizontal or oblique. If a shape can be cut in half by a plane with one half the reflection of the other in the plane, the shape has a plane of symmetry. A cube has nine planes of symmetry. A cuboid with no square faces has three planes of symmetry. A cuboid with two square faces has five planes of symmetry. The ability to identify the planes of symmetry in three-dimensional shapes draws upon the children's confidence in using mental imagery.

Preparation

Make a cuboid with one pair of square faces from Plasticine or play dough. Copy photocopiable page 105 for each child.

Resources needed

Plasticine or Play-doh, knives, mirrors, cubes, cuboids, triangular prism, tetrahedron, square pyramid, cylinder, cube, interlocking cubes, transparent acetate sheet, photocopiable page 105.

What to do

Use two wooden cubes and a piece of overhead projector transparency film to help define a plane of symmetry. Explain that a plane is a flat surface and ask the children to think of some examples of planes. Walls and mirrors are good examples. Then introduce the idea of a plane of symmetry by telling the children that a plane of symmetry divides a three-dimensional shape into two congruent halves in the same way that an axis of symmetry divides a two-dimensional shape. If you show the children two cubes, agree together that they form a cuboid and then slip the acetate between them; a clear demonstration of a plane of symmetry is given.

Reinforce this by using the previously prepared Plasticine model of a cuboid. Choose a child to demonstrate and then ask the other children to tell him where to cut the cuboid in order to produce two identical halves. After one cut has been made, check by reflecting one half in a mirror.

Ask the children to explore the planes of symmetry of a range of three-dimensional shapes by making small Plasticine models and cutting them. They should work with one shape at a time, trying to find all the ways it can be cut to produce reflecting halves. The children should try to find all the planes of symmetry for cubes and cuboids before moving on to triangular and hexagonal prisms. Encourage them to predict before cutting and draw their attention to the fact that a plane of symmetry will also produce a line of symmetry on two opposite faces. This is a useful way to check whether a plane of symmetry has been identified.

Introduce photocopiable page 105. The children use Plasticine and possibly mirrors to find the number of planes of symmetry for each three-dimensional shape. There is no need for them to draw the planes on the sheet as this is difficult and can confuse, but it is a good idea to check the children's understanding by asking them to indicate the planes of symmetry after they have completed the sheet. The challenge to make models with a given number of planes of symmetry is not as easy as it looks. Children may well produce large models with too many planes of symmetry. If this happens encourage them to identify a plane of symmetry which they nominate as 'extra' and find a way to disturb this plane without altering the others – they may just need to remove one cube. Smaller models can be easier to work with. As an alternative you could ask them to make, say, five different models with two planes of symmetry.

Suggestion(s) for extension

Extend the activity using interlocking cubes to make models with one, two and four planes of symmetry by playing a game. The children work in pairs, each child making a model with two planes of symmetry. They then remove a cube so that

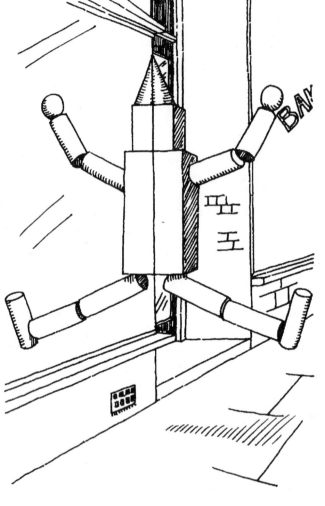

the model now has only one plane of symmetry and give it to their partner who has to replace the missing cube so that the model is returned to a state in which it has two planes of symmetry.

Ask the children to investigate the planes of symmetry of pyramids and other polyhedra. Encourage them to find vertical, horizontal and oblique planes of symmetry wherever possible. Some shapes have an infinite number of planes of symmetry. It is sufficient for the children to be able to identify the more obvious ones but you will need to monitor their work to check that they are 'looking' vertically, horizontally and obliquely.

Suggestion(s) for support

It is a good idea to stress the idea that a plane of symmetry cuts a solid shape and produces equal halves. Fruit such as apples, oranges, pears and bananas can be used to illustrate this before moving on to work with more obviously mathematical solid shapes. Limit the children to working with cubes and cuboids and proceed slowly. It is a good idea to offer the children a structure with which to work: start by checking for, say, any vertical planes of symmetry in a cube and a cuboid, and then any horizontal ones so that the children work systematically. The sloping planes of symmetry are likely to be the source of most confusion. Encourage the children to handle the shapes, holding them at different angles. By doing this they will re-orientate the shape so that what was oblique now becomes vertical or horizontal and most children identify these planes of symmetry more easily.

Ask the children to find examples in the environment of things with no planes of symmetry and things with one or more planes of symmetry. They can sketch them or write their names.

Assessment opportunities

Observe the children as they work and note individual children's responses to questions that you ask. Do they understand that three-dimensional shapes have planes of

symmetry? Can they identify the symmetries of simple three-dimensional shapes? Can they cut solid shapes to illustrate their symmetries? Do they understand the link between the lines of symmetry on the face of a three-dimensional shape and a plane of symmetry?

Display ideas

Ask the children to show the planes of symmetry on some three-dimensional shapes by cutting squares out of acetate with a suitably shaped hole in the middle into which the shape is inserted to illustrate one of its planes of symmetry.

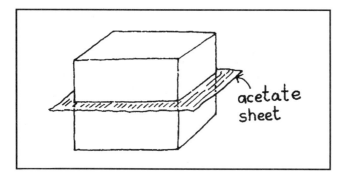

acetate
sheet

Reference to photocopiable sheet

Photocopiable page 105 gives three different shapes and asks the children to state the number of planes of symmetry for each one. The answers are:

(a) 3

(b) 4

(c) 9

The children are then challenged to use cubes to make models showing one, two and four planes of symmetry.

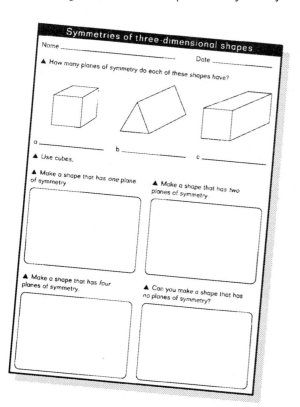

SPOTS AND NETS

To construct nets for irregular three-dimensional shapes. To use isometric paper to represent three-dimensional shapes.

†† *Small groups of 4–6 children followed by individuals.*

⏲ *60–120 minutes.*

Previous skills/knowledge needed

The children should be able to use protractors, set squares and rulers when drawing two-dimensional shapes accurately. They should know how to make the nets of three-dimensional shapes.

Key background information

The use of isometric paper to represent three-dimensional shapes requires that children use the structure given by the position of the dots to help them to draw. This is challenging for many children and it is important that they are given opportunities to engage in exploratory drawing. The design and construction of the nets of irregular shapes builds upon the ability to make nets for less complex three-dimensional shapes.

Preparation

Before the children undertake this activity they must have at least two opportunities to try drawing shapes on isometric paper. Cubes are the simplest but encourage them to develop their representations of cubes into cuboids by adding layers in different directions.

Resources needed

Interlocking cubes, isometric dotty paper, photocopiable page 106.

What to do

This activity is likely to require more than one lesson devoted to it. Ask the children to draw three-dimensional shapes on the isometric paper. Ask them to choose a simple shape based on cubes and then build it using interlocking cubes. As the children work, discuss the fact that some cubes can be 'hidden' when a shape is drawn on the paper. When they have completed their models, get the children to choose an edge on the model and find the corresponding edge on their drawing, then repeat this with the vertices. This will help you check whether they can link the representation and the model. Join four cubes in a line to form a cuboid and ask the children to draw the shape on the isometric paper.

Once you are sure that the children are using the paper correctly, introduce photocopiable page 106 and explain the task to them. They can either make as many four cube models as they can before moving on to draw them, or draw each model as they make it. The way of working should be their decision.

SHAPE, SPACE
AND MEASURES

When the children have finished, discuss their work with them. See if you can match drawings to models. Ask them to choose one of their simpler models and drawings and ask them to make the net for it. They should then choose a more difficult one to make. Encourage the use of rulers and set squares to construct accurate models. It is a good idea to tell the children to shade the faces on the net to help them keep track of their work.

Suggestion(s) for extension

Provide a variety of isometric and squared paper. Ask the children to draw different three-dimensional shapes. Make sure that models of the shapes are available. It is fun to use commercial packaging so that the children can illustrate their drawings to replicate the packages. This requires that they consider the scale of their drawings. It is important that the children make their own decisions about the most appropriate paper to use to draw a particular shape.

Suggestion(s) for support

If the children are struggling to work with the paper it may be because they are confused by the orientation of the edges of the shape. Encourage them to draw one cube and then put another on top of it, modelling this with the actual cubes. They should spend a great deal of time exploring the paper before representing the models and some may find it easier to use isometric paper which has lines rather than spots. Some children actually find it easier to draw the possible shapes first. Encourage this, as the skill of using the paper will gradually develop, so that they can move into making two-dimensional representations of solid shapes.

Assessment opportunities

There will be many opportunities for observation as the children work on this activity. Can they use isometric paper to draw a picture of their three-dimensional models? Can they identify the edges and vertices of models on their drawings and vice versa? Can they make the nets of their models? How accurate are the measurements of their own models?

Opportunities for IT

With some drawing packages it is possible to set up isometric grids, or for children to use intermediate points on square grids to draw their own three-dimensional shapes.

Display ideas

Ask some of the children to display their drawings and supply a pile of interlocking cubes. Other children can look at a drawing and try to build a model from it using the interlocking cubes provided. Display some of the nets on card along with the models and challenge children to match a model to a net.

Reference to photocopiable sheet

Photocopiable page 106 asks the children to build models using interlocking cubes and then represent them on isometric spotty paper. It then asks them to choose two of their models and make the nets for them.

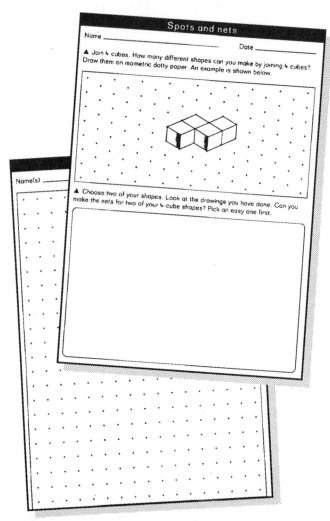

SHAPE, SPACE AND MEASURES

Two-dimensional shape

The names and properties of two-dimensional shapes are more familiar to adults than those of three-dimensional shapes. Much of the geometry that we studied involved the construction of regular polygons with mathematical instruments and sometimes we make the mistake of calling three-dimensional shapes by the name of their two-dimensional faces, for example mistaking a cube for a square or a rectangle for a cuboid. In working on both two-dimensional and three-dimensional aspects of shapes we need to teach children to think spatially as well as to name shapes.

The naming of a shape is likely to be dependent upon familiarity with that specific label rather than a knowledge of the mathematical properties of the shape if the only activities that the children experience have a narrow focus. Therefore we need to ensure that children learn how to make and construct shapes, to see how particular shapes fit together with themselves and other shapes, to identify similarities and differences as part of classification, and to develop an understanding of mathematical ideas such as angle and parallelism. Much of the work that children tackle in the context of shapes is laying foundations for more advanced learning in the fields of area and volume.

Two-dimensional shapes have two dimensions: length and width; some two-dimensional shapes are polygons. A polygon is a two-dimensional shape with straight lines. A regular polygon has all its sides the same length and all of its angles are equal. Children are generally most familiar with the regular polygons. It is important that they learn to recognise and use irregular polygons too.

FOLD AND COUNT

To make irregular polygons by folding. To visualise two-dimensional shapes.

†† *Individuals.*

🕐 *20–30 minutes.*

Previous skills/knowledge needed

The children should be able to recognise and know the names and properties of the common two-dimensional shapes such as squares, rectangles, triangles, pentagons and hexagons.

Key background information

The ability to recognise irregular shapes as belonging to the same set as regular ones is important. A child who sees that a polygon with all six sides and angles of different lengths and sizes is a hexagon has probably understood the main mathematical properties of a hexagon and almost certainly has a better understanding of shape and space than the child who only recognises the regular hexagon.

Preparation

Prepare scrap paper by asking a child to cut out squares, rectangles and triangles. You will need enough for each child to have one of each. Photocopy page 107 for each pair of children.

Resources needed

Scrap paper, paper for display, photocopiable page 107.

What to do

Revise the names of two-dimensional shapes with the children. As you talk about each shape remind the children about the importance of counting the number of sides it has, to establish its identity. Explain that a shape with all its sides the same length and all its angles the same size is called regular, for example a regular hexagon. Ask the children to show you what an irregular pentagon, hexagon and octagon might look like by sketching on scrap paper.

Take a rectangular piece of paper and fold it anywhere, opening it up before the children have a chance to see the resulting shape. Show them the rectangle with the fold line and ask them what the paper will look like when it is folded over. Encourage the children to use appropriate words to describe the shape, the length of the sides and the size of the corners or angles. Ask them to imagine the new shape and count the number of sides. This is challenging. After

you have listened to any responses ask a child to fold the paper along the fold line and count the number of sides. What is the new shape called? It is a good idea to draw the outline of the new shape on the board after counting the sides of the folded paper as some children do not realise that they should count around the outside of the whole shape.

Next each child uses their own rectangle and makes a fold that is different from your original one. How many sides does their new shape have? Ask them to compare theirs with a neighbour's. How are they the same? How are they different? What are their new shapes called?

Explain the task on photocopiable page 107 to the group. The children try to make shapes with four to nine sides by folding a rectangle. They then present their results as clearly as possible. Encourage them to write about their results. Which shapes were the hardest to make? Could they make some shapes in more than one way? Talk to the children as they make their displays and encourage them to present their work as clearly as possible so that others can understand what they have found.

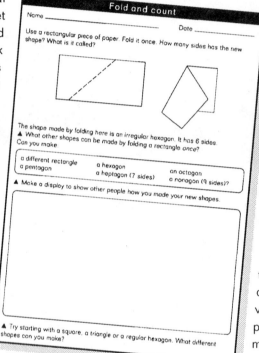

Suggestion(s) for extension

The challenge at the bottom of photocopiable page 107 is designed to provide children with an extension activity. Encourage the children to visualise the shape before they fold the paper. Questions like 'How could you make a pentagon with one fold?' can be used.

Suggestion(s) for support

Use thin card for folding. If the children have trouble keeping track of the number of sides in a shape suggest that they run their fingers around the outside of the shape, counting out loud. Alternatively they could draw around the shape and number the sides. This will help those children who want to count 'extra' sides.

Assessment opportunities

Observation of children as they work will provide evidence of their ability to visualise shapes. Ask questions to elicit descriptions of the shapes to help make judgements about their use of mathematical language. Do they use everyday words to describe the features of the shapes or do they use mathematical terminology? How accurately do they use mathematical language? Can they name irregular shapes? Can they visualise and predict the result of folding their paper? Do their displays communicate their findings clearly?

SHAPE, SPACE AND MEASURES

Display ideas
The activity has a display element built into it to help the children develop their ability to present information and results clearly. This work can be displayed on the wall or perhaps put into a book.

Reference to photocopiable sheet
Photocopiable page 107 provides the starting point for the paper folding activity. Suggestions for extension are included.

TWO CUTS

To visualise, describe and name two-dimensional shapes. To create different polygons by cutting a square. To use the properties of shapes during an investigation.

✝✝ *Individuals.*

🕓 *45–60 minutes.*

Previous skills/knowledge needed
The children will need to have worked with and know the mathematical features of common two-dimensional shapes. These should include squares, rectangles, triangles and some quadrilaterals.

Key background information
Children need to experience exploratory activities of an investigative nature in order to help them pose their own mathematical questions. This activity helps to develop their mental perception of shapes and requires that they use their knowledge of the properties of shapes in order to create different polygons, although the children may not realise that they are doing this!

The identification of similarities and differences in spatial work has its own special characteristics because of the need to consider reflection and rotation.

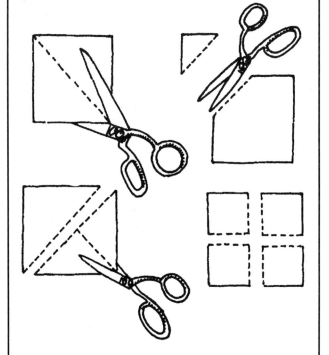

If you move a 'cut' a small amount in one direction, two identical isosceles triangles can become one isosceles triangle and one quadrilateral; the realisation that the isosceles triangles were congruent may only arise if the child recognises that they are the same shape in different orientations.

Preparation
Photocopy page 108 for each pair of children. Cut out some large squares from paper.

Resources needed
A mathematical dictionary, rulers, large squares of paper, wallpaper scissors or any large pair of scissors, acetate sheets, photocopiable page 108.

What to do
Show the children a large square and hold the scissors as if you are going to cut across the square. Tell them that you will start cutting where the scissors are and show them where the scissors will end up. Ask them to tell you what shapes the two pieces of paper will be. Discuss the possibilities briefly and then go on to carry out the cut. Repeat the process with another square. Encourage the children to name the shapes and describe them using appropriate mathematical terms to describe the shapes, angles and sides.

Introduce photocopiable page 108 and explain the activity to the children. They should experiment to start with and then choose their own starting point for investigation. Some possibilities for questions which you might ask to help children formulate their own lines of investigation include:

Can you make a triangle?
Can you make three triangles?
Can you make an isosceles triangle?
Can you make all the types of triangle?
What's the largest possible number of squares you can make with two cuts?
Can you make a pentagon?
If you make a hexagon, what other shapes are also made?
What if you make a rule that says your cuts shouldn't cross each other? What if they must?

An important part of this activity is the requirement that the children find a way to display their results clearly. Encourage them to tell the story of their investigation. What did they decide to investigate? How did they go about it? What strategies did they use? What did they find out? What might they do next? Encourage them to use the mathematical dictionary to find out the names of their new shapes if they are unfamiliar. The process of considering whether the properties of the new shape matches those of the shapes in the dictionary is very valuable.

SHAPE, SPACE AND MEASURES

Suggestion(s) for extension

Ask the children to investigate overlapping shapes. They can use acetate sheets and draw two congruent triangles, one on each sheet. They then use these to explore the polygons that can be made in this way.

Suggestion(s) for support

Limit the children to working with only one 'cut'. This activity could be carried out using acetate rather than paper to help the children see the effect of changing the position of their cuts. Draw a square on plain paper and draw a straight line across one acetate sheet which is larger than the square. Keep the square still and place the acetate sheet on top of it. The square will be divided into two parts by the line on the acetate sheet. The children should then explore with these materials before beginning to record their work.

Assessment opportunities

There will be much evidence from the children's recording. Can the children name the shapes that they have created? Do they differentiate between different types of triangles? Do they recognise irregular polygons? Do they work systematically, for example by keeping one cut in the same position and experimenting with the position of the other cut? Can they present their results in a clear and organised way?

Opportunities for IT

Each child or pair of children could take it in turns, either during or after the investigation, to use a drawing package to display their work. They could draw the shapes and then fill each of the new ones, created by cutting the original one,

in a different colour. Labels could be added to identify the names of each of the new shapes.

More able children investigating overlapping shapes could use a drawing package to help them explore resulting shapes and display their work. They can be shown how to create different geometric shapes and use the colour fill options to highlight the new shapes they have created. They could also use the text facilities of the drawing package to display the number of sides and the name of the new shape.

Display ideas

This investigation leads to work that makes an attractive display. The children can colour each section of the squares differently. Ask the children to cut the squares out and find a way of sorting them. The challenge is then for other children to guess the rule used for the sorting.

Reference to photocopiable sheet

Photocopiable page 108 offers examples of shapes made on squares by two cuts. It asks the children to explore other shapes that can be made.

FIND THE SHAPE

To introduce the idea of congruence of simple shapes.
To identify congruent shapes.
†† *Small groups and individuals.*
🕐 *30–45 minutes.*

Previous skills/knowledge needed

The children should be able to name and recognise common two-dimensional shapes. They should have had experience of making and describing them. The shapes used in this activity can be altered to fit the children's previous experience.

Key background information

Shapes are congruent if they are identical in every respect: length and number of sides, size and number of angles. Their positions and orientations may be different. Two shapes are similar if they are the same 'shape' but differ in size. Two regular hexagons of different size are similar.

Preparation

Prepare a 'feely bag' containing shapes such as squares and rectangles of different sizes, regular hexagons, different types of triangles. Make up a set of identical shapes to those in the bag. Photocopy page 109 for each child.

Resources needed

A number of two-dimensional shapes (squares, rectangles, triangles, hexagons), a 'feely bag', copies of photocopiable page 109.

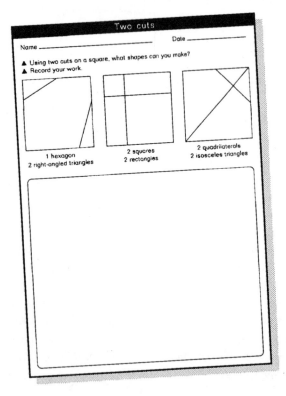

Two cuts

Name _____ Date _____

▲ Using two cuts on a square, what shapes can you make?
▲ Record your work.

1 hexagon
2 right-angled triangles

2 squares
2 rectangles

2 quadrilaterals
2 isosceles triangles

What to do

Show the group two identical triangles, placing them on the table in different orientations. Ask the children to talk about the similarities and differences between the shapes. They should identify that both triangles are exactly the same in every respect apart from their position. Ask how they could check to see whether they are the same, suggesting that they put one triangle on top of the other if this idea does not come from the children. They may well suggest measuring the sides and angles too. If this suggestion is made, ask the children to carry out the measuring. Explain that we can describe two or more shapes as congruent if one can fit on top of the other exactly, or if they are exactly the same shape and size. Ask the children to pick out some triangles from the set on the table that are congruent to those that you have shown them. Ensure that the children check by measuring or placing the triangles on top of each other. Continue by working with other shapes, asking each child in turn to pick out a shape congruent to one that you hold. Choose two shapes that are similar but not congruent and discuss them with the children.

Now show the children the contents of your 'feely bag' and ask them to pick out an identical set of shapes, so that there are pairs of congruent triangles of different types,

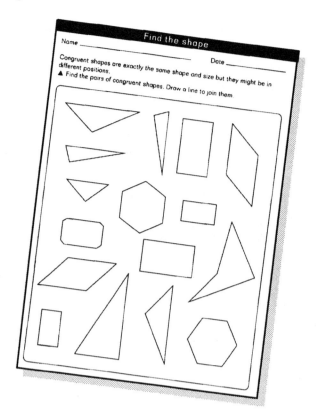

squares of different sizes, rectangles of different sizes and hexagons. Play 'Find the shape'. The children take turns to pick a shape from the set on the table. They then put their hand in the feely bag and try to take out the congruent shape. When a child removes a shape from the bag ask him to explain why he chose that particular one, encouraging him to talk about the number and length of the sides, and size of the corners or angles. Replace the shape in the feely bag, but remove the congruent shape from the table before moving on to ask the next child to choose a shape from the table and find its partner in the bag.

When every child has had one or two turns explain the task on the photocopiable sheet. The children should join the congruent shapes with lines. Remind the children about the earlier conversation in which congruence was defined.

Suggestion(s) for extension

Alter photocopiable page 109 so that some shapes do not have a congruent partner. The children identify those shapes that do not have a partner and draw a shape congruent to each one.

Suggestion(s) for support

The children should find congruent shapes in the environment. Ensure that they realise that objects can be different in colour or be in different positions but still be congruent by encouraging the children to fit them on top of each other. Encourage them to look at the outline of shapes.

Assessment opportunities

Ask the children to explain how they know that a pair of shapes were congruent. Do they check by fitting one on top of the other or by measuring? Can they recognise congruent shapes? Can they draw congruent shapes in different positions?

Display ideas

The children can create designs using congruent shapes in different positions and orientations. These could be made by sticking shapes on to paper or by using one shape as a template and using a crayon to rub over the edges of the shapes.

29

SHAPE, SPACE
AND MEASURES

Reference to photocopiable sheet

Photocopiable page 109 provides an assortment of polygons, both regular and irregular in different positions. The children identify congruent shapes and join them.

TRIANGLES

To identify equilateral, isosceles and scalene triangles and know their properties.

†† *Group then pairs.*

🕑 *35–50 minutes.*

Previous skills/knowledge needed

The children should be able to draw and identify triangles and other simple polygons. They should be able to identify whether an angle is more or less than a right angle.

Key background information

These are the properties of triangles:

An equilateral triangle has three sides with the same length. The angles are all 60°.

An isosceles triangle has at least two sides with the same length. It has two angles which are the same size. An equilateral triangle is a special sort of isosceles triangle which has all three sides and angles equal.

A scalene triangle has three sides of different lengths.

A right-angled triangle has one angle of 90°.

The internal angles of a triangle all add up to 180°.

Preparation

Collect a number of triangles from a mathematical set or prepare some yourself from card. You will need a variety of all types of triangle. Photocopy page 110 for each child.

Resources needed

Geostrips, cards labelled 'equilateral triangles', 'isosceles triangles', and 'scalene triangles' each having a picture of the relevant triangle, triangles (equilateral, isosceles and scalene), photocopiable page 110.

What to do

Distribute the geostrips and show the group an equilateral triangle. Ask the children to join three geostrips to make an equilateral triangle. Discuss its properties, highlighting the fact that the sides and angles are equal. Repeat this process with the isosceles and scalene triangles. Place the cards on the table to remind the children of the names and properties of the triangles. Discuss the properties of the triangles with the children, emphasising the differences between the lengths of the sides. Ask the children to work in pairs for two or three minutes, each holding up a triangle for the other to name and describe.

Introduce photocopiable page 110 to the children. They should join the diagonals of each shape first and then look for triangles created by the diagonals. They should colour each type of triangle a different colour. They do not have to colour in all the regions created by the diagonal lines, to do so would be confusing, but monitor the children as they work to ensure that they are finding triangles of all types.

Suggestion(s) for extension

Ask the children to find out whether isosceles, scalene and equilateral triangles tessellate. They can draw around shapes, fit them together or choose an appropriate mathematical paper to test their ideas.

Suggestion(s) for support

Simplify the task by asking the children to search for equilateral and isosceles triangles. If they have trouble identifying them it is a good idea to suggest that they turn the paper around. They may be able to 'see' an isosceles triangle that is standing on its base more easily than one that is lying on one of its sides or on its point.

Assessment opportunities

Observe the children as they work and ask them questions in order to elicit whether they have absorbed the properties of the triangles. As this may be their first experience of working with isosceles and scalene triangles it will be necessary to check again on another occasion to be sure that they have learned their properties. Can the children name the triangles? Can they find triangles on the photocopiable sheet? Can they describe triangles in terms of the their angles and sides? Do they use appropriate terminology correctly?

Opportunities for IT

The children could use LOGO to draw triangles, either directly on the screen or by using a repeat command. They could

start by exploring the idea of turn and the number of degrees in a right angle, possibly by drawing squares. They could then use the *sum of the angles of a triangle equals 180 degrees* to ensure that the sides of the triangle meet. They will also need to estimate the FORWARD movement to ensure that the sides will meet. They could be introduced to Pythagoras' Theorem in right-angled triangles as a means of drawing the triangles. More able children could go on to write procedures to draw triangles, possibly using variables to draw a range of different triangles.

Children could also use a drawing package to explore whether the different type of triangles tessellate. It will be

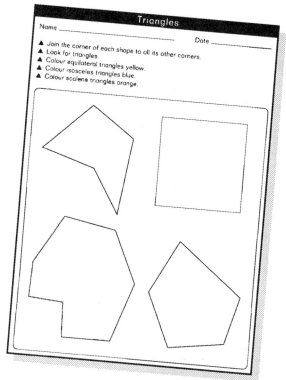

helpful to turn on the background grid and *snap to grid* facility for this work. An initial triangle can be drawn and then copied to make multiple copies of the original. This can be done by cutting the shape once and then pasting it back several times.

The children can then be shown how to move, rotate, flip and position each triangle to see if a tessellating pattern can be made. Extra copies of the original triangle can be made as needed, or the children can make copies of triangles already in the right orientation and simply 'drag' the copy to the new position. Each triangle can be filled with colour to make the final pattern more interesting.

Display ideas

The children can investigate the triangles made by joining the corners of regular shapes. These can be drawn using measuring instruments or templates on plain paper and the results displayed. Label the work with questions encouraging the children to look for shapes with specific triangles within them, for example, 'Can you find a shape with six scalene triangles?'

Reference to photocopiable sheet

Photocopiable page 110 provides irregular and regular polygons. The children are asked to join points to form diagonals and identify equilateral, isosceles and scalene triangles.

QUADRILATERALS

To identify the rotational and reflective symmetries of common regular quadrilaterals.

†† *Group then individuals.*

🕒 *45 minutes.*

Previous skills/knowledge needed

The children should be able to recognise and name squares, rectangles, parallelograms, rhombuses and trapeziums. They should know most of their properties. They should be able to find lines of symmetry by folding and should have worked on activities in position and movement involving rotation. They may know the reflective symmetries of squares and rectangles. They should be able to recognise whether a shape has rotational symmetry but do not need to be able to identify the order of rotational symmetry.

Key background information

These are the main properties of quadrilaterals:
A quadrilateral is a polygon which has four sides. The sum of the internal angles is 360°.
A rectangle is a quadrilateral with four right angles and opposite sides equal and parallel. It has two lines of symmetry and rotational symmetry of order two.
A square is a quadrilateral which has four sides of equal length and four right angles. It has four lines of symmetry and rotational symmetry of order four. It is a special type of rectangle.
A rhombus is a quadrilateral which has four sides of equal length, opposite sides are parallel and opposite angles are equal in size. It has two lines of symmetry and rotational symmetry of order two.
A parallelogram is a quadrilateral in which both pairs of opposite sides are parallel. It has two pairs of opposite equal angles. It has no lines of symmetry and has rotational symmetry of order two.
A trapezium is a quadrilateral in which one pair of opposite sides is parallel. It has no lines of symmetry. An isosceles trapezium is a trapezium which has one line of symmetry and one pair of opposite sides which are equal, this is the

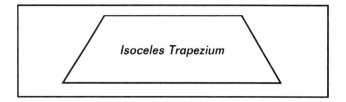
Isoceles Trapezium

SHAPE, SPACE
AND MEASURES

trapezium with which children (and adults) are the most familiar.

Preparation
Use thin card. Cut out a square, retaining the piece of card from which it has been taken so that a square-shaped hole remains. Mark one corner of the square with a large dot. Photocopy page 111 for each child.

Resources needed
Plain paper, thin card, scissors, mirrors, a set of different quadrilaterals (squares, rectangles, parallelograms and rhombuses of different sizes, isosceles trapeziums), acetate for supportive activity, photocopiable page 111.

What to do
Use the squares, rectangles, parallelograms, rhombuses and trapeziums. Revise their names and make sure that the children know most of the properties of the shapes. They should be able to pick out a shape and talk about its properties, for example 'I know it is a parallelogram because these sides and these sides are both parallel with each other.'

Explain that shapes have other mathematical features as well as those that they have already discussed. These are the rotational and reflective symmetries of the shapes. Demonstrate how to find the axes of symmetry by folding. This will probably be a case of reminding the children of work done previously. Ask them to find, mark and count the axes of symmetry of a square. Make sure that they identify the diagonal axes as well as the vertical and horizontal ones.

Now use the card square and demonstrate rotational symmetry by fitting it back into its hole. The children will be able to see when it has returned to its starting point by watching the dot in the corner. Explain that the square has rotational symmetry of order four because it will fit back into its original hole four times (including the original position), or in four different ways. Explain that if a shape can fit on to its outline more than once it has rotational symmetry.

Introduce photocopiable page 111 and explain that the children are to find out about the symmetries of the different quadrilaterals on the table by folding, using mirrors and drawing and rotating shapes.

To test the shapes for rotational symmetry the children take a shape and draw round it to make a congruent shape on paper. They then find out the number of positions in which the shape will fit on to its drawing, covering it exactly.

Suggestion(s) for extension
Ask the children to create different patterns based on a hexagon with rotational symmetry of order six. If they start by drawing in some or all of the diagonals this will help, as will limiting themselves to using a small number of colours.

When they have all made some designs ask them to compare them. The children will enjoy working with octagons, and their designs may become more and more complex.

Suggestion(s) for support
Limit the children to finding the reflective symmetries of the shapes and tackle the rotational symmetries at a later date in order to avoid confusion between the types of symmetries. Some children may fold their shapes to find an axis of symmetry and mark them in even though they are wrong, for example on a rectangle by folding from corner to corner. If this happens, they may well be confusing 'halving' with reflection. Ask the children to put a mirror on the axis of symmetry and look at the resulting reflection. If they are convinced that they are right because the action of putting the mirror on the line produces a shape with reflective symmetry (which it does!) they need to work with the mirror first and then fold to check. This means that you should ask them to experiment with the mirror until they find a position to place it where they can see a shape that is *exactly the same shape and size* as the original. They can then draw the mirror line and subsequently fold the paper.

The concept of rotational symmetry can be reinforced by using two pieces of acetate. Draw congruent squares on both pieces and use a brass paper fastener to join them at the centre of each square. Keep the bottom piece still while rotating the top square, counting the number of times that the top shape fits on top of the bottom one exactly.

Assessment opportunities
Observe the children as they work and look at the evidence provided by their recording on photocopiable page 111. Can they identify all the reflective symmetries of the

quadrilaterals? Can they test the shapes for rotational symmetry? Can they identify the rotational symmetries? Do they use the mathematical language correctly? Can they explain the reasons for the order of rotational symmetry of some shapes, perhaps comparing a square with a rectangle?

Opportunities for IT

The children could use LOGO turtle graphics to draw quadrilaterals on the screen. They can explore the need to ensure that the sum of the internal angles equals 360 degrees to draw closed shapes. Older or more able children could go on to draw different regular quadrilaterals using either a REPEAT command or procedures with variables.

The exact commands will vary depending on the version of LOGO used, but to draw a square of length 200 units requires something like:

```
REPEAT 4 [FD 200  RT 90]
END
```

This can be extended so that LOGO learns a new procedure called SQUARE. The procedure simply includes the REPEAT so that entering the command square would automatically draw the square with sides of 200.

```
TO SQUARE
    REPEAT 4 [FD 200  RT 90)
END
```

A further development would be to add variables so that squares can be drawn with different lengths of side. This is done using the command 'SQUARE :SIDE' where side is the length of the side of the square to be drawn. In this case the REPEAT loop within the procedure uses the variable 'SIDE'. The command SQUARE 400 draws a square with sides 400 units, SQUARE 50 draws a square with sides 50 units and so on.

```
TO SQUARE :SIDE
    REPEAT 4 [FD :SIDE RT 90]
END
```

A more challenging task would be to write procedures to draw rectangles or parallelograms. For a rectangle the REPEAT would be something like:

```
TO RECT :LENGTH :WIDTH
    REPEAT 2 [FD ;WIDTH RT 90 FD LENGTH RT 90]
END
```

Display ideas

The designs produced by the children working on the extension activity will make an effective and attractive display. Consider asking the children to copy their favourite design several times to make a tiling pattern.

Reference to photocopiable sheet

Photocopiable page 111 provides a chart which the children use to record the results of their tests for the reflective and rotational symmetries of the given quadrilaterals.

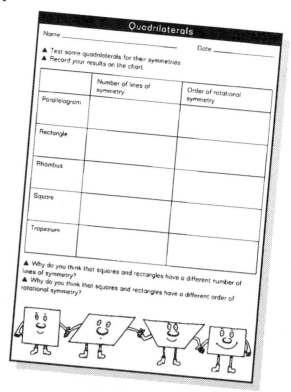

Quadrilaterals	Number of lines of symmetry	Order of rotational symmetry
Parallelogram		
Rectangle		
Rhombus		
Square		
Trapezium		

▲ Test some quadrilaterals for their symmetries.
▲ Record your results on the chart.

▲ Why do you think that squares and rectangles have a different number of lines of symmetry?
▲ Why do you think that squares and rectangles have a different order of rotational symmetry?

TURNING AND SHRINKING SHAPES

To investigate patterns made by drawing successively smaller two-dimensional shapes.

†† *Small group of 4–6 children.*

⏱ *45–90 minutes.*

Previous skills/knowledge needed

The children should be able to construct two-dimensional shapes such as squares, triangles and rectangles using set squares, compasses and rulers.

Preparation

Prepare one large example of each of the patterns shown on photocopiable page 112. A square is a good shape to use as a starting point. Photocopy page 112 for each of the children.

Resources needed

Set squares, compasses, rulers, templates of squares, triangles of different types, hexagons, octagons, photocopiable page 112.

What to do

This activity can be attempted in two parts if the teacher feels this would be more appropriate.

Show the group the first pattern created by joining the mid-points of the sides of the shape. Ask the children to offer ideas as to how the pattern has been constructed before showing them how to create similar patterns. It is important

SHAPE, SPACE
AND MEASURES

to ensure that the exact middle of each line is found, so stress the importance of measuring the length of the sides to find the exact mid-point. It is equally important that the shape is drawn accurately so the children should use the correct instruments properly when drawing the first shape which forms the outline. The marks identifying the mid-points should be as small as possible.

Now introduce photocopiable page 112 to the children. It provides a reminder as to how to create the pattern. The children should choose their own shape as a starter and use compasses, rulers and set squares as necessary to draw the first one. The larger the original shape the easier it is to construct the pattern. Check the children's work as they proceed to ensure that they are working accurately. When the children have become proficient they can attempt the off-centre patterns. In order to draw these accurately it is crucial to mark points that are consistently the same distance from each corner. It is helpful to turn the paper initially each time a new point is marked to ensure that the measurement is taken from the correct corner.

Once the children can draw both sorts of pattern they can experiment with different starting shapes.

Suggestion(s) for extension

Irregular shapes, for example scalene triangles, are more challenging to use as a basis for the construction of the off-centre patterns, as are those with a larger number of sides. Ask the children to measure the lengths of the sides of the shapes as they get smaller. By how much do they decrease each time? Can they explain why?

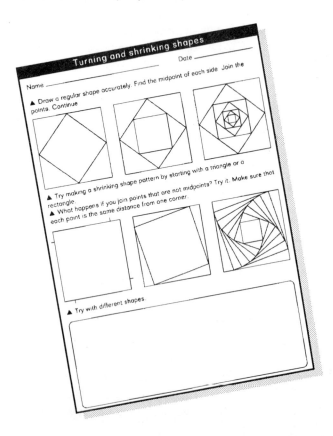

Suggestion(s) for support

The children should work with the pattern involving mid-points. They will find it easier to construct if they turn the paper each time as they draw a new shape. Some children find it easier to draw the smaller shape on a different coloured piece of paper and then stick it on to the new one.

Assessment opportunities

Observe the children and review the outcomes of their activity. Can they use mathematical instruments to construct the starting shape for each pattern accurately? Can they use a ruler to find the mid-point of a line? Can they construct patterns by successively joining mid-points? Can they construct patterns based on joining points that are off-centre?

Opportunities for IT

The children could use a drawing package with both the *background grid* and *snap to grid* facilities turned on. They could then use the line drawing tools to make a square and then draw internal squares from the mid-points of the sides. The editing and undo facilities of the drawing software enable the children to correct and edit their work as they go.

Alternatively children could use the TURTLE graphics part of LOGO to draw similar shapes, experimenting with procedures. In this case a simple TO SQUARE procedure can be written with a variable SIDE. Depending on the version of LOGO used it might look something like:

```
TO SQUARE :SIDE
    REPEAT 4 [FD :SIDE RT 90]
END
```

The children need to work out how to move the turtle to the new starting position so that it draws the next square in the right direction. These instructions could be included within the procedure.

```
TO SQUARE :SIDE
    REPEAT 4 [FD :SIDE RT 90]
    FD :SIDE/2
    RT 45
END
```

The next step would be to work out how long the new SIDE needed to be for the next square. Once this has been done this can be put into the procedure as well. The final challenge would be to write a single procedure which automatically draws a whole set of internal squares.

Ideas for display

All patterns constructed make attractive display items, especially if each new shape is drawn in a different colour. If some children work on the support activities the patterns made using different coloured paper should also be displayed.

Reference to photocopiable sheet

Photocopiable page 112 shows how to construct two variations of a pattern by drawing similar shapes that have smaller dimensions.

Position and movement

An understanding of the language of position, movement and angle is an important part of developing spatial awareness. Children learn to describe their own positions and those of objects through play and structured activities which help them to develop their ability to use positional language accurately. One of the most important things they realise is that position is relative. As they grow older they begin to recognise that a triangle remains a triangle even though it might have been moved in different ways.

Significant emphasis is now put on transformation geometry. The transformations studied involve a change of position and/or orientation without any change in size. Children work with three transformations: translation (sliding), reflection (flipping) and rotation (turning). In learning about transformations through easily performed actions such as folding, reflecting in mirrors and turning, children begin to develop a more intuitive appreciation of geometry.

The notion of symmetry is fundamental to an understanding of shape and other areas of mathematics. Young children often seem to possess an understanding of reflective, or line, symmetry which is evident in their drawings and models. The concept of rotational symmetry is more demanding and, in the early stages, is best approached through pattern-making and experimentation. The knowledge and skills that children gain through making patterns is applied in their work on properties of shapes where they classify, for example, rectangles according to their reflective and rotational symmetries as well as by their sides and angle properties.

SHAPE, SPACE AND MEASURES

TILE PATTERNS

To use rotation to create patterns. To visualise movements and develop the use of mathematical language to describe patterns.

†† *Individuals and pairs.*

🕐 *45–60 minutes.*

Previous skills/knowledge needed

The children should have had experience in using sliding and turning movements but they do not need to know the terms rotation or translation. Experience in working with materials such as the Association of Teachers of Mathematics tiling generators or other commercial tiling equipment would be useful but is not essential.

Key background information

Rotation involves turning a shape or an object about a fixed point. Any shape that fits on to its own outline more than once when turned has rotational symmetry. This activity involves children in identifying turning movements and using appropriate mathematical language to describe how they have been used to create patterns.

Preparation

None needed.

Resources needed

Interlocking cubes, 2cm squared paper, plain paper, colouring pencils.

What to do

Ask the children to choose up to three colours of cubes to work with and use them to make some different 2 × 2 square shaped tiles, for example:

They should then choose one that they consider most attractive and copy this design on to the 2cm squared paper, making eight identical tiles.

Let the children experiment with their tiles to create patterns for about ten minutes. Encourage them to make rectangular blocks rather than arranging their tiles haphazardly.

When you want to move to the more structured part of the activity ask the children to lay their tiles out in a 4 × 2 array, each tile facing the same way, for example:

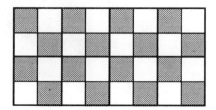

Ask the children to rotate the top row of their tiles a quarter turn or through a right angle. If they have been introduced to degrees as a measurement of turn ask them to turn the tiles through 90 degrees. Introduce the term 'rotate' for turn if the children have not met it before. Ask them to work out how many times they will have to rotate the tile following the same rule before it returns to its original position. Use the terms clockwise and anti-clockwise.

Ask the children to return the tiles to their original positions, all facing the same way, and then tell them that you want them to create a pattern by rotating their tiles in a systematic manner. One way would be to rotate every other tile through 90 degrees, another might be to turn each tile a quarter-turn more than the one before, another to turn one row through 90 degrees and the second row through 180 degrees and so on. They should keep their pattern hidden from their partner. When their patterns are complete they should copy the pattern accurately on to squared paper.

The next stage of the activity involves each child in helping their partner to recreate their pattern using verbal instructions. In order to prepare for this they should write a list of instructions which they can then read out for their partner to follow. It is a good idea to suggest that they use a step-by-step format, for example:

1 Put the tiles in two rows.

2 Make sure that they are all facing the same way with the red square in the top right hand corner.

3 Start with the first tile in the top row and turn it a quarter-turn/90 degrees clockwise.

SHAPE, SPACE AND MEASURES

When their instructions are complete each child should give his partner the set of tiles and read out the instructions. If they have to modify their instructions as they work in order to make the task easier for the partner they should note down any changes that they have made. Once both children in a pair have followed each other's instructions they can prepare a final version.

Suggestion(s) for extension
Ask the children to use their eight tiles to create two different larger tiles, each having rotational symmetry. If the children have not yet created shapes with rotational symmetry explain that a shape with rotational symmetry will fit back into its shape, looking exactly the same, at least once before it has completed a full turn.

Suggestion(s) for support
Give the children a very simple set of instructions to follow which will help them to learn and use the correct vocabulary then simplify the task by limiting each rotation that the children make with the tiles to 90 degrees. Work closely with them and discuss their work, encouraging them to tell you what they are doing in simple terms, for example 'I've got to turn the next tile a quarter-turn to the right (or clockwise).'

Assessment opportunities
There will be opportunities during the activity to observe whether the children can articulate the movements that they have made with their square tiles. The written explanation of how to create their patterns will provide further opportunities. Can the children identify a turning movement and can they say how much a shape has turned, either using degrees, right angles or quarter and half-turns as a measure?

Can the child describe the shapes and movements made clearly? Can the child follow a partner's instructions, visualising the shapes and movements?

Opportunities for IT
When the children are familiar with the idea behind this activity they could use a drawing package to design the components of their simple tile, adding colour to it and then combining all the parts as a single object. This can then be duplicated by 'cutting and pasting' it back to the drawing area several times. The individual copies can then be positioned by rotating and dragging them on the screen. If the software has a 'show grid' and 'snap to grid' facility this will help the children to design and line up the geometrically accurate shapes they have created.

The tiles the children have created can be used in the second part of the activity. The children could print out the pattern each time that an instruction is completed and then display the pattern alongside a word processed list of instructions. The finished patterns can be printed for display.

Children might also like to experiment with specific software such as *Kudlian Soft's RepTile* or *My World 2* with the *Tiling Generator* file to extend these activities.

Display ideas
Display the children's finished work along with questions encouraging them to compare patterns and look for similarities and differences.

PIECES

To construct two-dimensional shapes with reflective symmetry. To recognise reflective symmetry in irregular and regular shapes.

†† *Individuals.*

🕑 *30–45 minutes.*

Previous skills/knowledge needed
The children should be able to identify some of the reflective symmetries of simple two-dimensional shapes such as squares, rectangles and hexagons. They should be able to identify axes of symmetry by folding or using mirrors.

Key background information
This activity is open-ended and investigative in nature. The ability to create shapes with symmetrical properties builds upon the understanding of reflective symmetry and provides the children with opportunities to use and apply that understanding. Some children will be quite adept at identifying the symmetries of shapes but may find it more of a challenge to design their own, particularly when they are working with shapes with which they are unfamiliar.

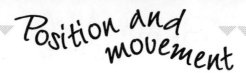

Preparation

Prepare a set of pieces identical to the ones that the children will use by photocopying and cutting out the pieces from photocopiable page 113. Make one copy of sheet 113 for each child, preferably onto thin card but otherwise onto paper.

Resources needed

Scissors, a variety of mathematical paper (spotty, squared, isometric), photocopiable page 113.

What to do

Show the children the three pieces that you have cut out from photocopiable page 113. Ask them to tell you how they could be combined to make a new shape. As they make suggestions tell them that the pieces must join along edges and must not overlap. The pieces can be flipped over or turned around. Follow their instructions and each time they suggest a shape, draw it on the board or on a large sheet of paper which has been divided in two by a line. Shapes having reflective symmetry should be drawn on one side and asymmetrical shapes drawn on the other side. Do not tell the children why you are doing this but explain that you are sorting them as you go, and ask them to the identify the rule that you are using to sort. Elicit from the children the observation that all shapes to one side of the line are symmetrical, or tell them if they do not realise after a while.

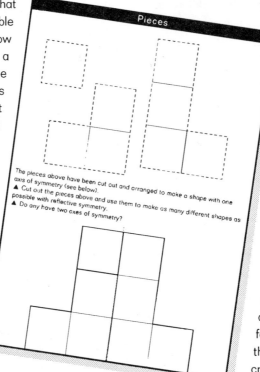

Pieces

The pieces above have been cut out and arranged to make a shape with one axis of symmetry (see below).
▲ Cut out the pieces above and use them to make as many different shapes as possible with reflective symmetry.
▲ Do any have two axes of symmetry?

Explain the task on photocopiable page 113. The children must use all three pieces each time they create a new shape. Encourage them to explore the possibilities of the shapes for the first five minutes or so and then move them on to work specifically on finding shapes with symmetry. Whilst they are engaged in the exploratory part of the activity you could encourage them by asking questions like: 'Can you make a long shape?' 'How is this shape different from the last one that you made?' 'Can you make a shape with no bits sticking out? How?' When the children move on to the actual task they should record their symmetrical shapes on paper or in their books if you prefer. Encourage the children to choose a grid paper or spotty paper which will enable them to produce the best representation. Making choices about the materials to use for a task is an important aspect of the decision-making aspect of using and applying mathematics. Remind the children to look for more than one

axis of symmetry in each shape. Ask them to show the axis of symmetry by drawing a dotted line or dotted lines on their shapes.

After about twenty minutes ask the children to compare their solutions, identifying any that are identical. This will require them to identify rotations of the same shape and some children may need to turn their paper in order to manage this.

Suggestion(s) for extension

Ask the children to add one more piece to their set. They should decide themselves what this should be. Then ask them to create shapes with two or more axes of symmetry, recording as before. How crucial is the extra piece? Do they think that they will be able to make more or fewer shapes with two axes of symmetry but using one more piece?

Suggestion(s) for support

Some children may find it difficult to manipulate the paper pieces. If this is the case use two-dimensional shapes, for example pattern blocks, to do the activity. They may also build upwards using the blocks and this is fine. The pattern blocks are easier to manipulate but it is more difficult to record the results unless the children draw around them. It is not necessary for these children to record their work as the main objective of the activity is to create symmetrical shapes and identify the axes of symmetry.

Assessment opportunities

Can the children construct a range of shapes with one axis of symmetry? Can they construct shapes with two axes of symmetry? Can they suggest possible changes which would increase the number of axes of symmetry?

Display ideas

This activity provides a good starting point for a display. The children can copy out their three most interesting designs on to plain paper, measuring accurately. Some children could replicate their designs using a graphical program on the computer.

Reference to photocopiable sheet

Photocopiable page 113 provides the task and a set of pieces which the children can cut out and use to create symmetrical shapes. They can copy the shapes accurately on to card and then cut them out if you prefer.

SHAPE, SPACE
AND MEASURES

SHAPES AND MIRRORS

To complete unfinished reflections of shapes. To use mirrors to create shapes. To use geometrical relationships to solve problems.

†† *Individuals.*

⊕ *40 minutes.*

Previous skills/knowledge needed
Children should have used mirrors to reflect shapes and have experience of drawing the reflections of shapes about axes in different orientations.

Key background information
An image can be reflected in a horizontal, vertical or sloping mirror line. Research shows that children are more successful in reflecting about a vertical axis than a horizontal one, with the sloping axis the most difficult to contend with. Many children will ignore the slope in such cases and reflect vertically or horizontally. Many find it easier to identify the axis/axes of symmetry in a shape than to reflect shapes. Shapes having edges parallel to or perpendicular to a mirror line are easier to reflect. The use of mirrors for work on reflective symmetry should not precede activities involving folding and cutting. These findings suggest that children need to be given much more experience in using mirrors to develop an intuitive understanding of reflection and that they require specific guidance in dealing with some aspects of reflective symmetry, such as coping with oblique lines.

Preparation
Make one copy of photocopiable page 114 for each child.

Resources needed
Two-sided mirrors, centimetre squared paper, triangular grid paper for the extension activity, photocopiable page 114.

What to do
Start by giving the children an opportunity to experiment with the mirrors. Ask them to colour four squares, joining edges or corners. They should then place the mirror in different

positions relative to the shape, creating horizontal and vertical mirror lines, and observe the effect. Encourage them to notice that the reflection is the same distance from the mirror line as the original object, that the further away the mirror is from the object, the further the reflection appears from the object.

Go on to ask the children to experiment by placing the mirror *on* their coloured squares and to observe the effect. They will probably block off much of the shape and then move the mirror backwards and forwards, making the shape look larger and smaller. Encourage them to place the mirror in different orientations and to look in both sides of the mirror. Help them to compensate for the natural tendency to work with the mirror held vertically on the page by encouraging them to rotate their mirrors through a range of angles. Ask the children to place their mirrors anywhere on their coloured squares and predict how the image and reflection will look.

Now explain the tasks on photocopiable page 114 to the children. Let them ask any questions in order to clarify any misunderstandings. For the first part of the activity they should place the mirror on the mirror line, observe the reflection and then complete the drawing. Some children will be able to manage this without using a mirror, but do encourage them to check with mirrors.

The second part of the sheet asks the children to place the mirror on a shape in different orientations and positions in order to create new shapes. This builds upon the earlier exploratory work, developing it so that the children use their understanding to achieve specific goals. This is challenging. Some children will manage the task through experimentation while others may develop a feel for the correct position of the mirror without being able to articulate their method. One approach is to identify an axis of symmetry on the new shape, place the mirror upon it and then take the mirror to the original shape, placing it on the corresponding position while keeping the mirror at the same angle. It is better if the children discover this for themselves rather than being told the method as much of the value of the activity will be lost if they do not experiment with different mirror positions.

SHAPE, SPACE AND MEASURES

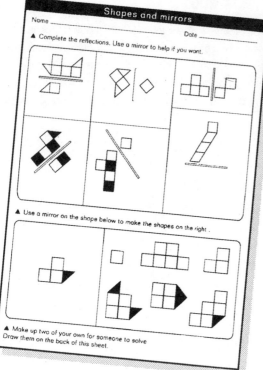

Shapes and mirrors

Name _____ Date _____

▲ Complete the reflections. Use a mirror to help if you want.

▲ Use a mirror on the shape below to make the shapes on the right.

▲ Make up two of your own for someone to solve
Draw them on the back of this sheet.

lines but you will need to observe them as they work with mirrors in order to make judgements about further use of mirrors. How do the children use mirrors? Can they work with vertical, horizontal and oblique mirror lines? Can they reflect shapes without using mirrors? How do they use the mirrors to create new shapes?

Display ideas
Use the work produced by the children doing the extension activity. Mount their work on card and invite children to use mirrors to make their shapes.

Reference to photocopiable sheet
Photocopiable page 114 is in two parts. It offers shapes and part-reflections which the children complete using mirrors as necessary. They are then asked to place a mirror on a given shape in different positions and at different angles in order to create specific shapes.

The challenge to create two new shapes demands that the children draw their new shapes. They will need to take particular care in drawing the lines so that the lengths are correct and in drawing the angles accurately. This is not as easy as it looks!

Suggestion(s) for extension
Use triangular grid paper and ask the children to shade four triangles. They can then create their own sheets by experimenting with the mirror to make new shapes and recording them. You can ask them to colour each triangle a different colour to make it slightly easier. Ask the children to swap sheets and re-create each other's shapes by using the mirror.

Suggestion(s) for support
Some children will find these activities challenging, and it will not always be those that you predict! While they are working on the first part of the photocopiable sheet check that the children are viewing the correct reflection and that they are not looking at the reflection of the part-completed shape. Help them to complete their reflections by pointing out that the reflection of each corner of a square is the same distance from the mirror line as the original. This means that they can complete the reflection by plotting the points at the corners behind the mirror line and then joining them up. If they have difficulty in working with reflections involving horizontal or slanting mirror lines suggest that they turn the paper so that the mirror line is vertical.

Assessment opportunities
The initial part of the photocopiable sheet will provide evidence of the children's ability to reflect shapes in mirror

STRIP PATTERNS

To use reflection and translation to create patterns. To analyse and describe patterns in terms of the transformations used to make them. To explore patterns from other cultural traditions.

†† *Pairs.*

⏱ *60 minutes.*

Previous skills/knowledge needed
Children should know and be able to use the terms vertical and horizontal. They should have worked on activities involving reflecting (flipping) and translating (sliding) shapes.

Key background information
African art has many examples of using patterned strips in carving or on cloth. All the patterns are made by combining

and repeating two sorts of transformations: translation and reflection about a vertical or horizontal axis. For example:

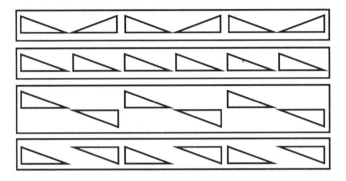

Preparation
Revise the terms vertical and horizontal with the children, making sure that they both understand and can use them. Revise the translation of shapes, using the term if it is appropriate. Make copies of photocopiable page 115 for each pair of children.

Resources needed
Card, scissors, colouring pencils, photocopiable page 115.

What to do
Ask the children to draw and cut out a triangle similar to those on photocopiable page 115. This is a scalene triangle with all sides of different length. Draw the first two strip patterns from the 'Key background information' section on the board and ask the children to identify the differences between the two patterns, discussing how they have been created. Encourage the use of appropriate mathematical terminology such as vertical, horizontal, flip, slide, translate. Encourage the children to use their own triangles to work out how the patterns have been created.

Explain the tasks on photocopiable page 115. The children should explain how the strips were made. In order to do this most of them will need to use their own card triangles, flipping and sliding them and probably drawing around them too. They can describe the strip patterns in sentences or by drawing and labelling diagrams. The search for an appropriate form of communication is an important part of using and applying mathematics. Once they have done this part of the activity they should try to find as many different strip patterns as possible. Limit them to the use of reflection and translation but acknowledge the contribution of any child who notices that a reflection through two axes can be made by rotating a shape. Encourage the children to use 'double reflections' which involve, for example, reflecting a shape horizontally and then vertically as in the third and fourth examples in 'Key background information'.

Suggestion(s) for extension
Ask the children to provide written instructions for making one of their patterns. They can then swap instructions and draw each other's pattern. How accurate were the instructions?

Suggestion(s) for support
Do not use photocopiable page 115 with the children, but concentrate on creating patterns by flipping and sliding the triangles. Start a pattern and ask the children to copy and continue it. Encourage them to predict the effect of a transformation, perhaps by sketching their prediction and then moving the triangle on to it to check for accuracy.

Assessment opportunities
The children's responses to the task on photocopiable page 115 will provide some written evidence for you to use when making judgements about the children's ability to use translation and reflection to describe patterns. Can they use both translation and reflection to create patterns? Are they able to visualise and describe the effect of reflecting and translating a shape? Can they see that a triangle has been reflected both horizontally and vertically? Can they find new patterns?

Opportunities for IT
The children could use a drawing or art package to extend this work. They will need to be shown how to create the different shapes and then to use the available commands to rotate or flip the shapes before building a pattern with them. The final results can be printed out and used for display purposes. The concept of drafting is an important one in this activity as children can correct mistakes or alter their strip patterns just as they would do with written work on a word processor.

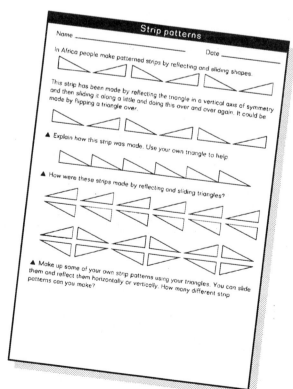

SHAPE, SPACE AND MEASURES

Display ideas

The work generated by this activity will make an attractive display. Ask the children to choose their favourite pattern and copy it neatly, continuing it along the length of an A4 sheet of paper. If these strips are mounted and the instructions for making the pattern written out separately the display can be used to ask the children to make instructions to strip patterns.

Reference to photocopiable sheet

Photocopiable page 115 provides the children with three different strip patterns and asks the children to describe how they have been constructed using translation and reflection. It then asks the children to construct their own strip patterns using the same principles.

FOUR IN A LINE

To use degrees to measure rotation. To develop accuracy in making and estimating angles. To use protractors to measure angles.

†† *Pairs.*

🕐 *30 minutes.*

Previous skills/knowledge needed

The children should be able to measure angles using protractors.

Key background information

There are two aspects to work on angles: static and dynamic. The static aspect of angle is concerned with the shape of a corner. It may be acute, obtuse, reflex or right-angled. An angle can be compared with a right angle on a set square or one made by folding paper, or a protractor. The dynamic version of angle is concerned with the measure of rotation and it is this aspect that is addressed through this activity. The angle made by the pages of a book with each other grows as the book is opened, or when a child stands with her arms outstretched together and gradually opens them.

The rotation of the minute, hour and second hands on an analogue clockface are good examples of dynamic angle and children can consider the angle the hour hand turns through in, for example, one hour, three hours, eleven hours or the minute hand in ten minutes, 30 minutes or an hour.

Preparation

Ask the each child to use card to cut out two card strips just over 1cm wide and 15cm long. They should connect two of the strips at one end using a brass paper fastener.

Copy photocopiable page 116 for each pair of children.

Resources needed

Card, scissors, brass paper fasteners, 360 degree protractors, counters, photocopiable page 116.

What to do

First ask the children to hold their strips vertically so that they line up with each other, with the brass fastener at the bottom. Ask them to turn the strip at the back through 90 degrees and to keep the front strip in its original position. They will have opened their strips to make a right angle. Now ask them to make angles of 180 and 270 degrees and check that they are able to do this accurately before moving on to the next part of the activity. Stress the idea that they are making the angle by turning one of the arms. Now ask them to make an angle that is less than 90 degrees and to estimate its size as accurately as possible. Discuss how they can check the accuracy of their estimates. Someone will probably suggest that they measure with a protractor. Ask them to make an angle as close to 45 degrees as possible by turning one of the arms and then get them to check using the protractors.

The next part of the activity involves using these ideas to play a game. The children take turns to choose an angle to make from the grid. If they are able to make the angle by turning one of the arms to within 10 degrees they claim the square by putting one of their counters on it, so after a child has made the angle her partner checks using the protractor. It is best if the strips are manipulated on the table so that

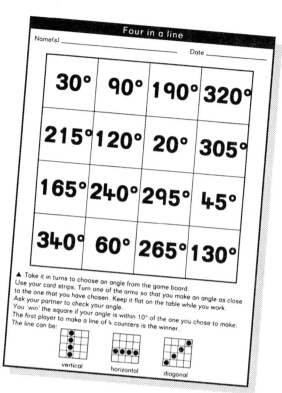

the angle does not alter once it has been set. The children continue to take turns until someone has made a line of four counters, diagonally, vertically or horizontally.

Suggestion(s) for extension

It is possible to make a harder version of the game by altering photocopiable page 116 so that the angles to be made are more demanding, for example by including more angles between 270 and 360 degrees.

Suggestion(s) for support

Limit the children to working with angles of up to 180 degrees. Draw some angles on paper and ask the children to use their strips to make an angle the same size by turning one of the arms. Stress the importance of keeping one of the arms in a vertical position and the brass paper fastener at the bottom at all times. Compare the angles that the children have made with those on paper.

Assessment opportunities

Observe the children as they work. Can they make estimates of angles to a reasonable degree of accuracy? Are they able to use protractors properly? Can they describe their angles using suitable terminology?

Opportunities for IT

A number of programs which children can use to practise estimating angles drawn on the computer screen are available. Some software can be set up to provide a range of angles and to record the outcomes of the activity.

Children could also explore angles using LOGO turtle graphics. They could experiment drawing different shapes

and angles; refining their initial estimates to guide the turtle around the screen or to draw particular shapes.

Alternatively the teacher could set up a course for the children to guide the turtle through, possibly a series of islands between which they have to steer the turtle, or even a boat. This island course could be created in advance and saved on to disk so that it can be loaded into the LOGO program for the children to use. Younger children could work on a similar activity using a large floor map and guiding a floor robot such as the Roamer or Pipp around the island in the shortest possible route.

Reference to photocopiable sheet

Photocopiable page 116 provides the children with a game which asks them to use paper strips to make angles by rotation to within a specific degree of accuracy.

COORDINATED SHAPES

To use coordinates to represent two-dimensional shapes. To transform shapes by translation on a grid.

†† *Individuals working within a group.*

⏲ *40 minutes.*

Previous skills/knowledge needed

The children should be able to plot points on a grid which has the lines numbered so that the coordinates relate to the intersections.

Key background information

Any point in space can be identified by using a system of coordinates. Being able to use coordinates involves the ability to be able to read both along and up. The first number (or letter) in an ordered pair normally indicates the point on the horizontal axis and the second is used to indicate the point on the vertical axis. Shapes can be translated by adding a constant number to the x- or y-axis.

There are four quadrants in which coordinates can be plotted. The first quadrant involves the use of positive numbers only, the second, a combination of positive and negative numbers, the third and fourth both use negative numbers.

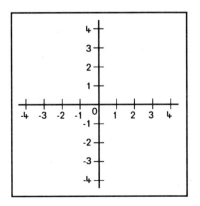

SHAPE, SPACE AND MEASURES

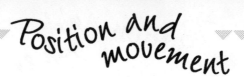
Preparation

None needed.

Resources needed

Centimetre squared paper.

What to do

Ask the children to use squared paper and draw horizontal and vertical axes, labelling the lines from 0. Check that they understand that points are plotted by finding the position on the x-axis first; the phrase 'along the corridor and up the stairs' is a useful one to use to jog the memory. Now ask them to plot the coordinates of a square, a rectangle and a triangle, recording the coordinates as ordered pairs separately. Check that the children have plotted the points and recorded the ordered pairs correctly.

Work with the group to demonstrate the next stage of the activity. Ask them to give you four points which can be joined to make a rectangle. Plot the points and record the ordered pairs. Now ask them to add 3 to the x-coordinates of each ordered pair and then plot the new points and observe the effect:

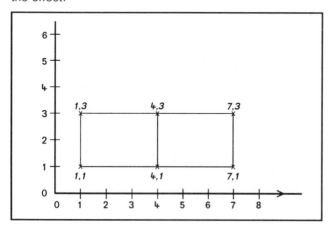

Discuss with the children what has happened and encourage them to explain why the shape has moved along. The children should now use a fresh grid, labelled in exactly the same way as their first and then replicate the process that you have demonstrated by adding 3 (the constant) to the x-coordinates of all their ordered pairs and plotting the points of each shape.

Now ask the children to experiment with this idea, adding different numbers to the x-coordinates of their ordered pairs and translating their squares, rectangles and triangles.

Suggestion(s) for extension

Ask the children what they will need to do in order to move the shape upwards on the grid (add the same number to the y-coordinate) and then let them experiment. What happens if they add the same number to each coordinate? The children can explore the effect of subtracting a constant from the x-coordinate which will involve translating the shapes in the opposite direction. This may open up the possibility of working

with coordinates plotted in the second quadrant and working with negative numbers, for example:

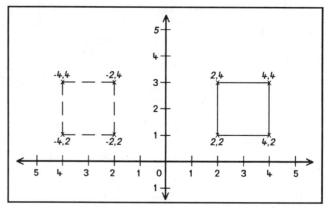

It might be a good idea to help the children understand this by drawing the shape where they want it to end up and work out what number has to be subtracted to move it there.

Suggestion(s) for support

It is important that the children realise that the same number must be added to each ordered pair. Ask them to plot one point separately, write down its ordered pair and then add 3 to it and plot it. This may help them to see that each corner of a shape is made up of a different point in space and the effect of altering these. If they still struggle with this idea, show them a square and its coordinates and then attempt to translate it by adding different numbers to the x-coordinates. The result will be somewhat perplexing and should help the children see the need for consistency.

Assessment opportunities

There will be written outcomes which can be assessed from this activity but you may need to ask the children some specific questions in order to gauge whether they have understood the notion of translation. Can the children plot coordinates correctly? Do they plot the x-coordinate first? Can they represent two-dimensional shapes using coordinates? Can they translate two-dimensional shapes by altering the coordinates? Can they predict the effect of altering coordinates? Can they translate the shapes horizontally? Can they translate the shapes vertically? Can they work with coordinates in the second quadrant?

Opportunities for IT

Children could use one of the many specially written programs which provide activities for plotting and using coordinates.

Children could also use the coordinate facilities of LOGO's Turtle graphics to plot shapes on screen using coordinates rather than directly moving the turtle through forward and turn commands. They will need to be shown how the coordinate system works, how the commands are entered and the range of coordinates that can be used on the screen.

SHAPE, SPACE
AND MEASURES

Length

Length is the measurement of a line which may be straight or curved. Children learning about length at Key Stage 2 are likely to have worked through a number of stages. These involve learning to compare the length of two and then three or more objects without measuring but through direct comparison. They will have learned to use non-standard units for measuring objects, such as matchboxes or books before recognising the need to use one standard unit for comparing objects so that measurements made are comparable. They will realise that if a line alters its position its length does not change. They will probably be at the stage of learning how to use standard units such as metres and centimetres to measure and compare objects and distances. This work involves two crucial skills: estimating with various units of measure and using the relevant measuring instruments.

The ability to estimate and measure relies to some extent upon an ability to develop mental models of some lengths and use them. For example, if we need to estimate how much carpet is required for a room we might pace out the distances in metres using our visual image of a metre to help, or we might use a known fact such as 'the kitchen is three metres wide and that side of the room looks about half a metre longer'. Both methods demand that we have built up pictures of lengths which can be called up when necessary to help in the measuring process. We can begin to develop this ability in children by giving them explicit opportunities to use and apply their own mental pictures whenever possible, checking their estimates against the actual measurements frequently.

SHAPE, SPACE AND MEASURES

RODS

To estimate and measure in centimetres. To use measuring instruments. To develop a visual model of some lengths to use when estimating and measuring.

†† *Small groups and pairs.*

🕐 *30–40 minutes.*

Previous skills/knowledge needed

The children should be able to estimate and measure using non-standard units. They should have seen the need for a standard unit for measuring lengths of less than a metre and may have had some experience in using centimetres already.

Key background information

Cuisenaire rods provide a visual model of the number system, each rod being a different colour and length. The colour names used for this activity are those of the Cuisenaire rods but their descriptions can easily be translated into those of the Colour Factor system or any other similar form of apparatus. This apparatus is particularly useful at the early stages of learning to measure because the length of each rod is exact. This activity will help to reinforce some basic number concepts as well as develop the ability to measure using centimetres.

Preparation

Each child will need a copy of photocopiable page 117.

Resources needed

Cuisenaire or Colour Factor rods or any similar mathematical apparatus, a ruler for each child, photocopiable page 117.

What to do

Start by showing the children a book and discussing how they would go about finding out how long or how wide it is. Remind them about any measuring that they have done using non-standard units. Ask the children to look at their rulers and demonstrate how to use them to measure the book. If they are using rulers with alternate coloured centimetre spaces they will need to begin by lining up the ruler with the

end of the book and counting the spaces. If they are using the more advanced type which has a space between the end of the ruler and the first mark you will need to show the children how to line up the object being measured with the first subdivision (which is, in effect, zero). Children will often measure from the '1' mark so it is important that at an early stage they are taught how to use the ruler correctly.

Distribute the rods and ask the children to measure their lengths and widths. They should establish fairly quickly that each rod is 1cm wide. Watch them carefully as they measure to ensure that they are using the rulers correctly. There should be no recording at this stage as the aim is to learn how to measure using standard units. Show the group a rod and ask them to find one that is shorter, then measure it and tell you its length. Encourage them to use mathematical language correctly, saying 'This rod is five centimetres long' or 'The length of this blue rod is nine centimetres.'

Ask the children to estimate the lengths of some of the rods but do not be too disappointed if their estimates are inaccurate. This will probably be due to the fact that they have not yet developed a mental image of certain lengths. The ability to estimate will improve as they continue to measure objects but it is important to encourage estimation wherever possible.

Go on to use the photocopiable sheet when you judge that they are ready to work unaided. Explain the task to them and give each pair a set of rods, with one rod of each colour. They should find the length of each rod first. Some may do this systematically by starting with the shortest while others will work in a more random manner. There is no need for you to make them work in order as the objective is to practise measuring. They then go on to find the total length of pairs of rods which are put together end to end. This part of the activity has an investigative element which you may want to exploit if some of the children finish quickly. You can ask them to find as many different combinations as possible using two rods.

Suggestion(s) for extension

Ask the children to draw lines of a given length. They could use the information from the first part of the photocopiable

SHAPE, SPACE AND MEASURES

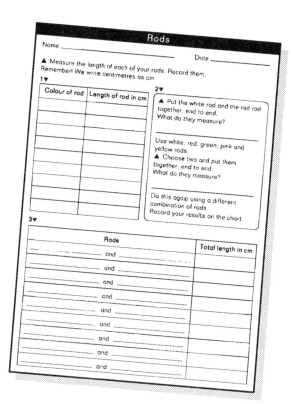

using two or three different coloured pencils. They should be drawn at random, crossing each other. Use the resulting patterns as a stimulus for questions like: 'Can you find a line on Simon's paper that is 10cm long ... shorter than 9cm?' 'Can you estimate the lengths of all the blue lines on Sian's paper?'

Reference to photocopiable sheet
Photocopiable page 117 provides the context for the second part of the activity and is for the children's recording.

MAKE A METRE

To use and apply knowledge of measuring length in solving problems. To use measuring instruments to measure in centimetres.

†† *Pairs within a large group.*

🕐 *20–30 minutes*

Previous skills/knowledge needed
Children should be able to measure in centimetres.

Key background information
This activity is designed to enable children to use and apply their knowledge of number and measures. They will tackle it in different ways. It is important that they are not told how to approach the problem but find their own methods of doing so. This question can be tackled by children who are at different levels of competence in number and measuring as it is possible to answer it by trial and improvement methods alone, or by using a combination of measuring and calculation to varying degrees.

sheet to draw a set of lines of the same length as their set of Cuisenaire rods. They can then evaluate the accuracy of their drawing by comparing each line with the relevant rod. Ask the children to use three or more rods if you want them to practise measuring longer lengths. This will help them to see that they do not need to 'count along' the ruler but can read off the number closest to the length of the rod.

Suggestion(s) for support
Work closely with the children to help them use the ruler correctly. It is a good idea to use the simpler form of ruler with children who struggle with this kind of work as they will be less likely to start measuring from the '1' subdivision. Ensure that they are familiar with early language such as 'longer than' and 'shorter than' and let them spend a good amount of time on finding rods that are longer than or shorter than others, measuring to check. This will help establish that measuring using rulers and other instruments takes place in a context in which there is a real need for their use.

Assessment opportunities
Observe the children as they work on the measuring activities and check their photocopiable sheets. Can they use the rulers correctly? Do they record the lengths of the rods correctly? How accurate are their measurements?

Display ideas
Ask the children to fill an A5 page with lines of lengths between 1cm and 20cm. They could draw one of each line,

SHAPE, SPACE AND MEASURES

Length

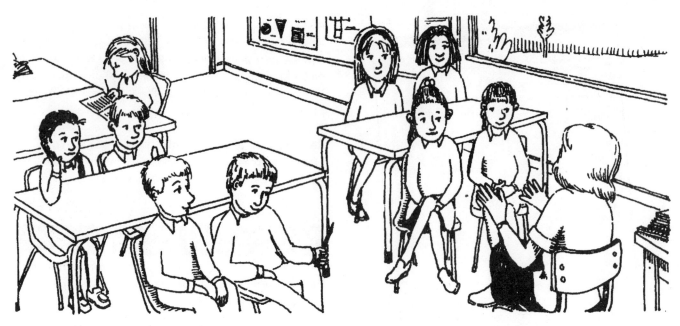

Preparation

The equipment and materials should be available but not distributed as the children should select their own equipment for this activity. Decide what size paper you are going to give the children to work with. A4 is very suitable but some of the children may find the task more accessible if they use A3. Make copies of photocopiable page 118 for each pair of children.

Resources needed

Plain paper, scissors, sticky tape, rulers, tape measures, metre sticks, calculators, photocopiable page 118.

What to do

Give a copy of photocopiable page 118 to each pair of children and explain that you want them to talk to each other for two minutes about the task and you will then answer any questions that they may have. After two minutes hold a brief discussion with the group but be sure that you do not tell the children how to go about tackling the problem. They will probably ask you questions about using certain items of equipment or whether there is a time limit.

After clarifying the task and answering any questions set the children to work. Be aware that if you give a time limit some children may struggle if they are not used to this sort of work. It is important that they are given opportunities to make mistakes and learn from them. Make sure that when the children are working you stand back and resist the

temptation to correct them too quickly as they may well find a better way of doing things without your help. There is, however, nothing more frustrating than asking for help and receiving no feedback at all so the following questions can be useful in helping the children to make progress without giving them too much guidance:

What have you done so far?

How long is this piece of paper?

How many times do you think it might fit along a metre stick?

How many smaller strips do you think you will need?

After about fifteen minutes stop the group and find out how they are getting on by asking some of the pairs to report on their progress. It is a good idea to choose children who you think will be able to offer others new ideas. You might want to write some 'handy hints' up on the board. You can then refer to them as you work with other children subsequently. You may want to clarify at this point whether you are going to allow 'overlaps' – this makes the task less demanding so some pairs might benefit from this method of differentiation.

The children are likely to finish the activity at different times. It is important to hold a discussion with the whole group when they have all finished to help the children to reflect upon their learning. Ask them to tell you about the things that they found difficult and those that they found easy. Get them to tell you how they overcame any difficulties and ask them how they would go about it if they were to do the same problem again. Encourage the children to identify

the mathematics that they used, for example some may have divided a metre by the length (or width) of the paper; some children may have multiplied the length of the paper by a number to see how close to 100cm they could get and then tried again, using a different number to multiply by. Some will have used addition in a less advanced way but it is important to acknowledge the rich variety of approaches used.

Suggestion(s) for extension

Some children may enjoy the challenge of being given a number of different-sized pieces of paper and writing a set of instructions that would enable them to make a metre strip from any of them.

Suggestion(s) for support

Work closely with the children initially. Encourage them to use a metre stick and compare it with their paper. Some children find it helpful to halve their paper along the length and to continue to do so until their strips can be laid along the metre stick.

Assessment opportunities

There will be many opportunities for you to observe the children as they work on the problem. If you choose to ask the children to write up how they went about the task there will be additional recorded evidence. Watch to see how they tackle the problem. Do they start to cut the paper immediately or do they measure its length and work out how many strips they will need to cut? Is their approach based upon 'trial and improvement' methods where they try to make a strip with little measuring and then use the outcome to inform the way in which they make the next one? Do they use rulers correctly when measuring? Can they perform calculations with length?

Display ideas

The resulting metre strips can be displayed along with any writing that the children produce.

Reference to photocopiable sheet

The photocopiable sheet presents the task and can be used by the children to explain how they tackled the activity. Its use is optional.

PATTERN BLOCK PERIMETERS

To find perimeters. To make shapes with a given perimeter.

†† *Individuals.*

🕐 *35–45 minutes.*

Previous skills/knowledge needed

Children should be able to estimate and measure in centimetres. They should have had experience of using pattern blocks.

Key background information

Children often confuse area and perimeter. Helping them to see the difference by using terminology such as the fence around the playground for the perimeter, and the playground for area can help to avoid misunderstandings from early on.

Preparation

Copy enough of photocopiable page 119 for every child to be able to see one. There is no need for them to have one each.

SHAPE, SPACE AND MEASURES

Resources needed

Rectangular box lids, string, small books, rulers, pattern blocks, isometric paper for recording, photocopiable page 119.

What to do

Demonstrate how to find the perimeter of a box lid, establishing that it is the distance around the face. Wrap a piece of string around the lid and cut it so that it is the same length as the perimeter of the top face of the box lid. Draw a diagram and label each side to show how the perimeter in this case is made up of four separate measurements which are combined. Check the measurement obtained in this way against the length of the string. Discuss the fact that opposite sides of rectangles are equal and encourage the children to find a quicker way of calculating the perimeter using this fact but do not introduce the formula 2 x (width + length) at this stage. Let the children find the perimeters of the box lids and books, drawing and labelling their diagrams.

Explain the activity on photocopiable page 119. Make sure that the children realise that they should make shapes by joining the pattern blocks along edges and not at corners or points. The children can use isometric dotty paper for drawing their shapes which can then be cut out, stuck in their books and labelled. In order to answer the questions on the sheet they will need to do a fair amount of experimentation, building shapes and measuring in order to find those with the longest and shortest perimeters. Some children will calculate the perimeter by keeping a running total mentally whilst others will break the process down into smaller steps, finding the length of each side and totalling them. Encourage the children to try both approaches, using one to check the other.

Discourage the children from drawing round the blocks, encourage them instead to measure the sides of the blocks and produce accurate representations of their shapes.

Suggestion(s) for extension

Use the pattern blocks to help the children see that shapes can have the same area but different perimeters. The children should choose five identical blocks and use them to make different shapes, recording their perimeters each time. How many different shapes can they make? (Exclude rotations of shapes.) Do any of the shapes have the same perimeter?

Suggestion(s) for support

Ensure that the children realise that the perimeter is the 'distance all the way round' the shape. If they have worked previously on finding areas of shapes they may use the wrong units of measurement and record perimeters as square centimetres. It is sometimes helpful to talk about perimeter using images such as: 'How far would a spider have to walk if it wanted to go for a walk all the way round the shape until it got back to its starting point?'

Use an orange square, a blue rhombus and a green triangle and ask the children to make different shapes first. They should keep each shape and when they have made, say, four different ones ask them to estimate which has the longest perimeter. Help them to draw each one and ensure that they record the length of each side. They can then find the total length of all the sides by adding in small steps.

Assessment opportunities

Observe the strategies the children use to find perimeters. Do they appreciate that perimeter is concerned with the

distance around a face or shape? How do they calculate perimeter? Can they record perimeters pictorially? How accurate are their drawings of the shapes made?

Opportunities for IT

The children could use calculators to work out the perimeters of their shapes, either by adding the lengths of the sides together or, once they have established a rule using it to work out the perimeter.

The children could also go on to use a spreadsheet to set out their findings and to get it to calculate the perimeters. The spreadsheet should be set up in advance by the teacher and children can enter their results as the activity progresses. If enough computers are available each group of children could work on their own spreadsheet.

The spreadsheet could provide a space for each measurement and then calculate the perimeter using a sum command or once the children have worked out a formula they could enter it as well (see column g). Extra columns could be inserted for shapes with more than 4 sides.

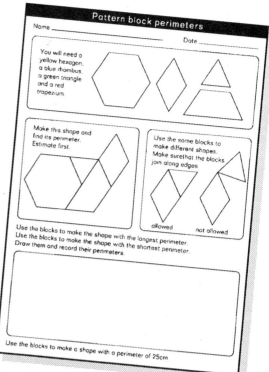

	a	b	c	d	e	f	g
1	shape	side 1	side 2	side 3	side 4	Perimeter	Perimeter
2	red square	4	4	4	4	sum (b2, e2)	b2 x 4
3	blue triangle	3	6	7		sum (b3, d3)	b3 + c3 + d3
4							

The activity could be extended to allow children to model with the spreadsheet to find the shape with the greatest perimeter. Using the formula sum (b2, e2) the children can insert figures in columns b, c, d and e to see which shape with four sides has the largest perimeter. Children should be shown how to replicate a formula down a column so that they can try out and keep the results of many examples.

Display ideas

Much of the resulting work can be displayed in the mathematics area and will look attractive. Use some of the children's solutions to the problems and mount them on card and then ask the children to put them in the order of the perimeter length.

Reference to photocopiable sheet

Photocopiable page 119 provides the activity for the children to work on when they have established a definition of perimeter and learned how to calculate it using measuring instruments.

SHAPE, SPACE AND MEASURES

SMALL OBJECTS

To estimate and measure objects using millimetres.
To translate between centimetres and millimetres.
†† *Small groups and individuals.*
🕐 *30–40 minutes.*

Previous skills/knowledge needed
Children should be able to measure using centimetres. They should have been introduced to decimal fractions and be able to recognise that a tenth of something is written as 0.1.

Key background information
The use of millimetres to measure length adds a greater degree of accuracy than is possible with centimetres. It leads to the use of decimal fractions in the context of measuring length as each millimetre is 0.1 or one tenth of a centimetre.

Preparation
Ask each child to bring in an empty matchbox a few days before you plan to do this activity. Make a copy of photocopiable page 120 for each child.

Resources needed
Matchboxes, rulers, scrap paper, small items to fit in a matchbox, photocopiable page 120.

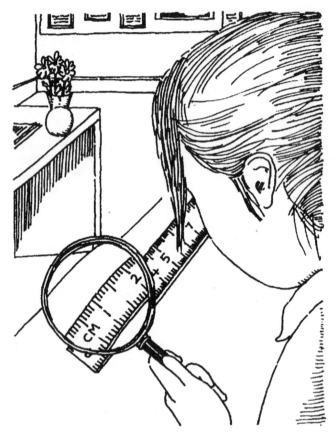

What to do
Each child will need a ruler and their matchbox. Show them the millimetres and get them to count how many there are in a centimetre. Ask the children to measure the width of their matchboxes, first in centimetres and then in centimetres and millimetres. Record some of their measurements on the blackboard and demonstrate how to write them so that the millimetre is expressed as a decimal fraction of the centimetre. It is a good idea at this point to remind them about any work they have done in decimals that will help them understand the relationship between centimetres and millimetres.

Ask the children to draw some lines of specific lengths on scrap paper using sharp pencils. Say the lengths in different ways, for example: 'three point two centimetres ... two centimetres and three millimetres ... nought point six

centimetres ... six centimetres and six millimetres'. Make sure that the children use the rulers correctly. Stress the importance of accuracy but be prepared to accept a certain degree of inaccuracy as it is very difficult to measure and draw lines to such specific requirements at this age. It is realistic to ask them to be accurate to 1mm but some children may find this challenging.

When you are fairly sure that the children can measure and draw using millimetres, distribute photocopiable page 120 and explain the activity to the children. Encourage them to be as accurate as possible during their measuring.

Suggestion(s) for extension
The children can work in pairs. One draws a line and the other estimates the length and then measures it. Encourage them when estimating to use language like 'just over three centimetres ... 5 and a half centimetres ... nearly six centimetres.' The measuring of the line after they have estimated will help them to appreciate the added accuracy that working with millimetres gives.

Suggestion(s) for support
Some children may find it difficult to use a ruler to measure in millimetres. Make sure that they are using the ruler correctly, measuring by using the first mark on the ruler as a starting point rather than putting the end of the ruler at one end of the object being measured.

Assessment opportunities
Observe the children as they work and check whether they are using the ruler correctly. Do they make a reasonable estimate of the length of the objects in centimetres and millimetres? Do they know that there are ten millimetres in a centimetre? Can they measure reasonably accurately in millimetres? Are they able to express a length in millimetres as a fraction of centimetres?

Display ideas
Display the contents of the matchboxes along with the matchboxes. They will provide a useful stimulus for measuring activities at odd times of the day when the children have

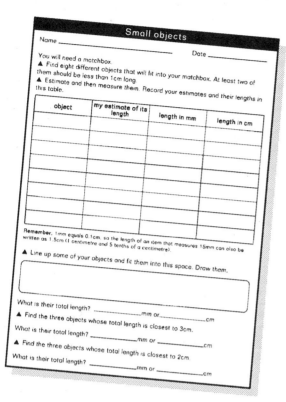

Small objects worksheet:

Small objects

Name _____ Date _____

You will need a matchbox.
▲ Find eight different objects that will fit into your matchbox. At least two of them should be less than 1cm long.
▲ Estimate and then measure them. Record your estimates and their lengths in this table.

object	my estimate of its length	length in mm	length in cm

Remember, 1mm equals 0.1cm, so the length of an item that measures 15mm can also be written as 1.5cm (1 centimetre and 5 tenths of a centimetre).

▲ Line up some of your objects and fit them into this space. Draw them.

What is their total length? _____mm or _____cm
▲ Find the three objects whose total length is closest to 3cm.
What is their total length? _____mm or _____cm
▲ Find the three objects whose total length is closest to 2cm.
What is their total length? _____mm or _____cm

finished other activities. Put up signs which encourage them to carry out further measuring, for example: 'Can you find three things that are all shorter than 2cm?' 'How many of the objects in Lizzie's box are longer than 3.2cm?' 'Take one object out of each box and find their total length.'

Reference to photocopiable sheet

The photocopiable sheet provides the task on which the children will work. It is also an aid for recording the measurements made in the course of the activity. Make sure that the children record their lengths both as mm, and cm and mm, for example, 14mm and 1.4cm.

MEASURE ME

To use metric and Imperial measures. To know the rough metric equivalents of Imperial units.
†† Small groups.
🕐 45 minutes.

Previous skills/knowledge needed

Children should be able to estimate and measure using a wide range of standard metric units confidently and accurately. They should be able to use and understand decimal notation in the context of measurement.

Key background information

The programme of study for mathematics requires that children should be familiar with both metric and Imperial units of measurement still in daily use, and this knowledge and understanding is listed at Level 5 in the level descriptions for Shape, Space and Measures. Although some Imperial units are becoming less common, an understanding of their use is still advantageous in daily life and the relationship between these units and metric ones can be an interesting and challenging area to study, both mathematically and historically. This activity focuses on yards, feet and inches and their relationship to metres and centimetres.

Preparation

Prepare and display a large chart showing the relationships within Imperial and metric units and display it on the wall a few days before you plan to ask the children to do the activity. Draw the children's attention to it and answer their questions or draw their attention to it informally.

1 kilometre = 1000 metres   1 mile = 1,760 yards
1 metre   = 100 centimetres   1 yard = 3 feet
1 centimetre = 10 millimetres   1 foot = 12 inches

Abbreviations: yd = yard
               ft = foot or feet
               in = inch/inches

Make a copy of photocopiable page 121 for each child, or enough for each child to be able to see one if they will be recording on paper or in books.

Resources needed

Rulers and tape measures showing both metric and Imperials units, photocopiable page 121 (if required).

What to do

Establish through discussion which Imperial units are still in use and encourage the children to think of situations in which they have seen them. Point out how some rulers will let you measure both in centimetres and inches and draw the children's attention to the fact that 30cm is roughly a foot. Ask the children to use rulers and tape measures to compare yards and metres, feet and centimetres and inches and centimetres. Encourage them to make comparisons between the units, such as 'a yard is shorter than a metre' as they work.

The next part of the activity involves the children in measuring various parts of their bodies using both systems, so when they have worked on the relationship between the standard units in both systems ask them if they know their height in feet and inches. If no-one does, tell them your height. Refer to your previously prepared chart and explain that there are 12 inches in a foot. Write your height on the board, using the correct abbreviations, for example 5ft 2½in (it is probably best to avoid the symbols ' or " at this stage).

Ask the children to suggest other measurements that could be taken: length of foot, distance from fingertips to elbow, handspan, circumference of head are all fairly popular and unlikely to upset those children who might be embarrassed by the activity. They should find five measurements in all and write them on the photocopiable sheet or draw a cartoon figure in their books and label that. When they have recorded five measurements they can then either convert them to metric units using calculators or by using measuring instruments to help.

When the children have finished measuring and converting hold a brief discussion in which you focus on the similarities and differences between measuring in both systems. It is a good time to remind them about the pattern in the metric system and its close links with place value.

Suggestion(s) for extension

Ask the children to draw a conversion graph for converting inches to centimetres.

Suggestion(s) for support

Some children may have difficulty with the fact that there are 12 inches in a foot and 3 feet in a yard. It sometimes helps if they make a 'yard strip' and mark off the feet and inches. They can then use this to measure with.

Assessment opportunities

There will be plenty of opportunities for you to observe the children as they work in order to ascertain whether they have made progress in learning about Imperial units. Can they name the Imperial units of length in discussion? Do they measure using Imperial units accurately and can they choose

appropriate units to measure with? Are they able to give the rough metric equivalents of yards, feet and inches?

Opportunities for IT

The children could use graphing software to record some of their measurements in both metric and Imperial units and use them to plot a line graph making a simple conversion chart. It may be necessary for children to use a similar conversion chart in advance so that they understand how they work. They could make different conversion charts in this way, for example inches to centimetres, miles to kilometres.

Older or more able children could use a spreadsheet to create an automatic ready reckoner where, when the metric unit is typed in, the Imperial answer is given automatically. Children will need to investigate a conversion formula in order to do this.

	a	b
1	Inches	centimetres
2	12	a2/2.54
3		
4	miles	kilometres
5	5	a5 × 1.6

— *conversion formula*

Display ideas

Make a display of artefacts and put rulers and tape measures that use Imperial units with them. Make a sign asking the children to find the dimensions of the objects on display. You could ask a child to draw a table onto which other children can record their measurements.

Reference to photocopiable sheet

The children can record their findings on the photocopiable sheet or work directly in their books or on paper.

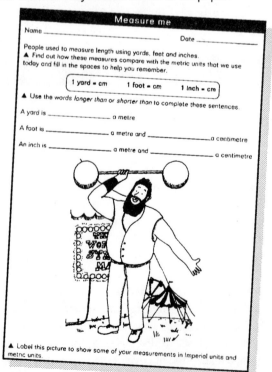

SHAPE, SPACE AND MEASURES

Area

Young children begin to learn about area as they cover up surfaces with shapes, painting and jigsaws, and valuable discussion can take place about comparisons of shape and size. Two surfaces can then be compared by fitting one on top of the other before the children use non-standard units first of arbitrary size and then of uniform size, to compare areas. The introduction of the square centimetre as a standard unit follows. As in other forms of measurement the concept of conservation is important. Some children will still need help to see that, for example, if pieces of card are rearranged on a surface, the area covered does not change even though the shape and position of the pieces has. This is vital if children are to go on to understand formulae such as 'the area of a triangle is half the length of its base times the height'. Tangram puzzles can help develop an understanding of the conservation of area.

Children often find the difference between area and perimeter hard to grasp, thinking that they are interchangeable. They need a secure understanding of area as a measurement of surface, measured by counting squares so early work on area should not include formulae based on lengths and widths. This should help avoid confusion with perimeter which is a linear measurement. Opportunities that involve investigating shapes with varying perimeters but constant areas will also help. The notation cm² should not be introduced until the children have a secure grasp of the square centimetre as the unit of measurement, as its similarity to the centimetre used to measure length is often a source of confusion.

SHAPE, SPACE
AND MEASURES

Area

RECTANGULAR AREAS

To find areas by counting squares. To investigate shapes with constant areas.

✝✝ *Large group and individuals.*

🕑 *30–40 minutes.*

Previous skills/knowledge needed

Children should have experienced activities which involve covering surfaces using non-standard units. They should be familiar with common two-dimensional shapes.

Key background information

In order to find the area of a surface it is necessary to work out the number of unit squares (cm^2) within its boundaries. The investigation of different shapes with the same area supports the development of understanding of conservation of area.

Preparation

Photocopy pages 122 and 123. Each child will need a copy of page 123, pairs could share page 122. Some children may use more than one of page 123 so have some spare copies available.

Resources needed

Geoboards and rubber bands, rulers, photocopies of pages 122 and 123.

What to do

Start by letting the children investigate the geoboards individually or in pairs if they have not used them before. Encourage them to use the bands to make squares, rectangles and triangles. You could ask questions like: 'Can you make a different square ... a bigger one?' 'What if the sides of that triangle were longer?' 'Which shapes are hardest to make?'

When you judge that the children can use the geoboards to make specific shapes ask them all to make a square. Ask them to compare their squares with those of their neighbours. They should concentrate on identifying the similarities and differences. This is best done by asking them to find three ways in which they are the same and then three ways in which they are different in turn if they are unaccustomed to working on similarities and differences. Establish that the properties of the square still remain the same (number of equal sides and corners) and that the length of the sides and area enclosed can vary.

Ask the children to tell you whose square they think is the largest. Suggest that they count the number of squares enclosed as a way of deciding. Encourage them to find a quick way of counting the number of small squares. Some will need to count in ones, but others should be able to find out how many in a row, for example six, and then count in sixes. Others may count the number of small squares in a row and then multiply by the number of rows. Do not tell the children to multiply the length of one side by the length of the other at this stage. It will confuse many children and may lead to them seeing area as a one-dimensional rather than a two-dimensional concept. Introduce the term 'area' as the children work on this part of the activity.

Ask the children for suggestions as to the size of the small squares used for measuring the area of the shapes. Introduce the term square centimetres and the notation cm^2 at this point.

Distribute photocopiable pages 122 and 123. Explain that they should start by looking at the rectangle with an area of $12cm^2$ and then try to find more rectangles that have the

Area

same area. Encourage them to visualise first. The children can use geoboards or work with pencil and paper. After they have worked on this task for a short time, check that they have understood the task, stressing that they should be measuring the size of their rectangles by finding their area. They can then work individually, finding rectangles with an area of 16cm², 8cm² and eventually choosing their own size of rectangles to investigate.

Suggestion(s) for extension

Ask the children to make a chart which shows which rectangular areas are possible and which are impossible. Can they explain why this is? Encourage them to think about links with multiplication facts.

Suggestion(s) for support

Less confident children will benefit from working on the initial activity using geoboards and finding the area of the shapes for a longer period of time. They can then work on finding as many squares with different areas as possible using the geoboards. It is important that the children have extended experience of counting the squares before moving on to record their findings.

Assessment opportunities

Observe the children and question them as they work on the activity. Can they estimate the area of a shape? Have they developed an efficient method for counting squares? Can they use the mathematical terminology to describe area? You will be able to assess whether they can find areas

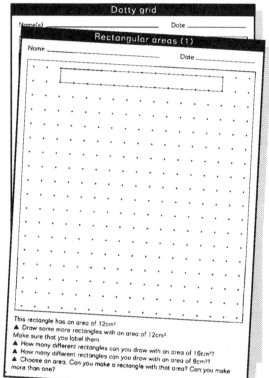

correctly from the children's written work. You will also be able to check whether they can find or draw shapes with the same area.

Opportunities for IT

Children could use a drawing package and create a 1cm square which they can then duplicate and use to build shapes of specific areas. If the software has a 'snap to grid' facility the children will find it easier to line up their squares properly. They could go on to fill the squares with colour and print their work to make an interesting class display.

Similar activities can be undertaken with framework software such as *My World 2* and the Maths support files.

Display ideas

Make a display showing shapes with the same area. Children can either cut out the shapes from their worksheets or make copies of them on to coloured paper, replicating the dimensions as accurately as possible by tracing or using rulers. The extension activity will provide a table which can be used as a basis for a display.

Reference to photocopiable sheets

Photocopiable page 122 gives the instructions for the written part of the activity. Photocopiable page 123 is dotty square grid paper on to which children draw and label their rectangles.

SHAPE, SPACE AND MEASURES

Area

SPLODGES

To find areas by counting squares, including part squares and to estimate and approximate areas.

†† *Large group and individuals.*

🕑 *30–45 minutes.*

Previous skills/knowledge needed

Children should be able to find areas by counting squares. They should be able to say whether more or less than a half of a square has been shaded.

Key background information

Previous activities in 'area' will have introduced children to the idea of using square centimetres as a standard unit of measure. Unfortunately, shapes and regions do not always come in neat, regular forms so it is necessary to find a way of measuring area when parts of squares are covered. This concept relies upon children understanding that measurement is approximate. Where children are measuring irregular shapes they need to learn to include any square of which half or more is within the area being measured. They should not count parts of squares which are less than half. This method will generally produce a satisfactory approximation by evening out differences.

Preparation

Using centimetre squared paper colour three irregular areas lightly. Ensure that parts of squares are covered. Photocopy page 124 for each child.

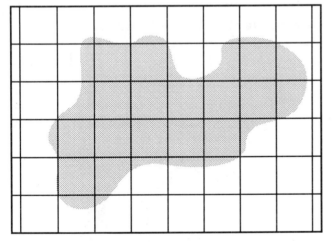

Resources needed

Centimetre squared paper, centimetre squared grids on acetate, either commercially produced or made by copying a grid on to an overhead projector transparency, colouring pencils, photocopiable page 124.

What to do

Show the children your prepared 'splodge'. Ask them to estimate how many squares are covered. You might like to show them the paper for about five seconds and then hide it

to encourage the children to develop their ability to use mental imagery. As you collect their estimates, encourage them to say 'about ... square centimetres' in order to stress the approximate nature of measurement. Encourage them to give their reasons for their estimate.

Tell the children that you need to find a way to check their estimates and discuss with them the problem of dealing with the part squares. Ask for suggestions and discuss the relative merits of each. This will give you an opportunity to assess how well they can use mathematics to overcome

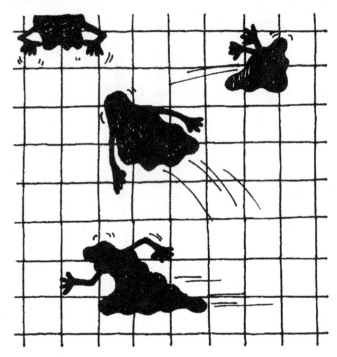

problems. Explain the convention that part squares of half or more are counted and that squares of less than half are ignored and that this will give an approximate answer. Go on to use this method to find the approximate areas of the other two splodges, asking the children to estimate first and then choosing a child to carry out the counting.

As the children become confident in using this method, provide them with photocopiable page 124 and ask them to find the areas of the splodges. When they have completed the sheet and if you are confident that they have understood the task, ask them to turn their paper over and draw some splodges on the back with colouring pencils. As there will be no squares on the plain paper show them how to use the acetate grid by placing it over the splodge in an appropriate position. Ask them to find the approximate area of each of their own splodges using the grid to help them count.

Suggestion(s) for extension

Children could investigate this method of counting squares further by cutting up splodges and fitting together part squares to test its accuracy. They could evaluate the accuracy of other methods and record the differences between methods.

SHAPE, SPACE AND MEASURES

Area

Suggestion(s) for support

Work closely with the children. This method relies upon the children having an understanding that if a shape is rearranged its area will still be the same. It also demands the ability to do some quite sophisticated counting by including some bits and ignoring others. You may need to work on the thinking behind the method by asking them to cut out the shapes and fit part squares together.

Assessment opportunities

As the children work on photocopiable page 124 ask questions like: 'What do you think the approximate area of this shape is going to be?' 'Can you tell me how you worked that out?' 'Do you think that this splodge is larger or smaller than this one ... why?' 'Which splodges was it easier to find the area of?' Can the children use the rule when dealing with part squares? Observe them as they work with the acetate grid. How do they use it to help them find areas?

Display ideas

The splodges can provide an interesting stimulus for display work with interactive questions asking children to find the areas, perhaps using grids. The children could draw splodges of an approximately constant area but with different dimensions.

Reference to photocopiable sheet

Photocopiable page 124 provides grid paper with a number of splodges superimposed. Children find the areas of the splodges. The back of the sheet is used for further work with the children drawing and finding the area of their own splodges. As an alternative to using the sheet for recording on the work can be done separately on paper or in books.

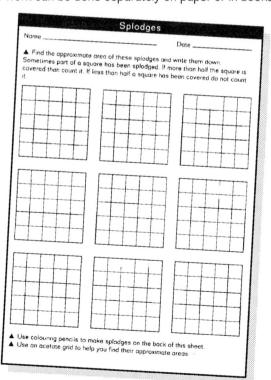

OUTSIDES AND INSIDES

To compare shapes with equal areas but different perimeters.

✝✝ *Individuals.*

🕐 *30 minutes.*

Previous skills/knowledge needed

Pupils need to be able to find areas by counting squares. They should understand and be able to find perimeters.

Key background information

Children frequently become confused between area and perimeter, particularly if they have not had sufficient experience of measuring area using geoboards and dotty paper which help them understand that area is a measurement of a surface or region. Shapes can be made which have equal areas but different perimeters, or equal perimeters and different areas to help them differentiate between the two concepts.

Preparation

Photocopy sufficient copies of photocopiable page 123.

Resources needed

Geoboards, photocopiable page 123.

What to do

Ask the children to make a shape with a perimeter of eight units on their geoboards. Ask them to compare their shapes and discuss the similarities and differences. Listen to the conversations and suggest that they compare areas and

perimeters if they do not do this of their own accord. You may need to remind them that perimeter is the length of the boundary, or outside. Ask questions like: 'Do both shapes have the same perimeter?' 'Do they both have the same area?' 'Which shape has the largest area?' 'Can you see another shape with the same area as yours?' 'Can you see a shape with a smaller area?' Ask the children to make another shape with a perimeter of eight units but with an area larger than their previous one.

When you are sure that the children are secure in their knowledge of the difference between area and perimeter, set the task. Ask them to find as many shapes as possible with a perimeter of 16 units. Each time they discover a new shape they should record it on the dotty paper. Ask them to find the shape which encloses the most space; this will be a 4 × 4 square. The shape which encloses the smallest space is the 7 × 1 rectangle. They can work directly on to the dotty paper if you, or they, prefer.

Suggestion(s) for extension
Children can investigate which shape has the largest area if the perimeter remains constant. They should cut out several pieces of string of equal length, for example 12cm or 16cm and then use small drawing pins or sticky tape to fix each piece of string on to squared paper to

make a different shape. They could make a square, a triangle, a pentagon, a hexagon, a decagon and a circle. They can work out the area enclosed by each shape and record it on a chart or table. They should discover that the circle is the shape which encloses the greatest area because the more sides in a shape, the larger the area. Encourage them to discuss the reasons for this.

Dotty grid

Name(s) _____ Date _____

Suggestion(s) for support
Work closely with the children. Ask them to work with a constant area rather than a constant perimeter as it is easier to make or draw a shape with, say, eight squares than it is to find different shapes, all with a perimeter of eight units.

Assessment opportunities
Assessment will need to centre around the children's ability to differentiate between area and perimeter. Can they explain the difference between the two concepts? Have they noticed that long thin shapes have a smaller area? Can they make a shape given specific instructions, such as 'a shape with a perimeter of 18cm and an area of 20cm²'?

Reference to photocopiable sheet
Photocopiable page 123 is dotty square grid paper onto which children draw their shapes.

SLICING SHAPES

To find the areas of shapes by methods involving dissection.

†† *Small groups and individuals.*

🕐 *30–45 minutes.*

Previous skills/knowledge needed

Children should be able to find the area of rectangles. They should be able to find areas on grids where fractions of squares are covered. They should understand that the area of a shape is not altered if it is dissected and pieces moved. They should have worked on activities with quadrilaterals.

Key background information

The area of any parallelogram can be found by changing it into a rectangle of the same area. The formula for finding the area of a parallelogram is therefore Area = base × height. The use of dissection as a method for finding areas relies in part upon the ability to visualise the movement of shapes by sliding, reflecting and rotating.

Preparation

Cut from centimetre squared paper a parallelogram of base 10cm and height 6cm. Photocopy sheet 125 for each child.

Resources needed

Centimetre squared paper, scissors, rulers, photocopiable page 125.

What to do

Start by showing the group the parallelogram. Discuss its properties (four sides, opposite sides parallel and equal in length, opposite angles equal) and then ask the children to estimate its area. Discuss their strategies for estimating, encouraging the children to explain how they came to their estimated answers. Encourage them to consider the number of squares in a row and the total number of rows in order to work more quickly.

Demonstrate that the parallelogram can be rearranged to form a rectangle by making one cut and rearranging the pieces by sliding the triangle:

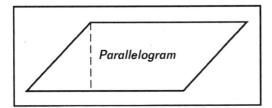

Parallelogram

Work with the children to find the area. Rearrange the pieces by sliding the triangle back across to form the original parallelogram and write down its base and height, then use the pieces to reconstruct the rectangle and record its base, height and area. When the children realise that both shapes

have the same area ask them to explain why this is. Ask the children to spend ten minutes trying the activity for themselves. They should cut out different-sized parallelograms, find their areas and then cut off a right-angled triangle and rearrange the pieces to make a rectangle. They should then find the area of the rectangle. The children could record this aspect of the activity by drawing the parallelogram with the cut line showing and then drawing the rectangle resulting from rearranging the pieces. They should label the base and height of each shape and ensure that their drawings are either life-sized or to scale.

Show the children photocopiable page 125 and ask them to point out the parallelograms. Show them an isosceles trapezium and ask them to talk to their partner about how they would find its area by cutting and moving pieces. Do not demonstrate how this might be done at this stage as the children will work on this problem individually. This dissection differs from the previous one in that the triangle created by cutting the trapezium has to be rotated, turned over and translated in order to create a rectangle.

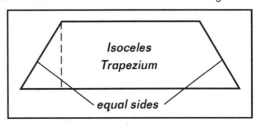

Isoceles Trapezium

equal sides

Finally, ask the children to tackle the questions on the worksheets individually as far as possible. They should estimate the area of each shape and then use dissection

SHAPE, SPACE AND MEASURES

squares. Remind the children to include any part of half or more and ignore parts that are less than half in order to make a good approximation.

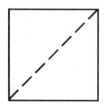

Assessment opportunities

Observe the children as they are working. Can they dissect trapeziums and parallelograms to form rectangles? How accurate are their estimates of the areas of shapes? Can they use formulas to find areas? Are they beginning to work towards a formula by stating a rule in words for finding areas?

Display ideas

A wall display can show examples of square dissections from the support activity or any of the dissections from the main activity. Include questions which encourage the children to look further at the display, perhaps by asking them to match dissections to the original shape by estimating the area.

Reference to photocopiable sheet

Photocopiable page 125 provides quadrilaterals for the children to cut out and find their areas. If you do not want to cut up the sheets, the children could copy the shapes on to squared paper and then cut them out. Some children will be able to do the activity by visualising and drawing, so stress the fact that dissections do not have to involve physical cutting.

methods to find the areas of all the shapes, recording their findings.

Suggestion(s) for extension

Ask the children to draw several congruent rectangles and use them to produce various trapeziums by dissecting them in different places. If the children know and can use the formula for the area of a rectangle then ask them to work out the formula for the area of a parallelogram ($A = b \times h$). They can then practise the use of the formula by drawing parallelograms, using the formula to calculate areas and then using the dissection method to check that their calculations are correct.

Suggestion(s) for support

Some children may benefit from more experience of rearranging a shape to make a new one to help them appreciate that they cover the same area. They could work on square dissections by first drawing a 5 × 5 square and finding its area. Then they can draw three horizontal and/or vertical lines and cut along them to form smaller rectangles. Ask the children to rearrange the pieces so that they touch along edges and then to calculate the area of the new shape by finding the area of each smaller piece and adding them all together. They should rearrange the same pieces several times and then work with another square with the same dimensions. This time they make two diagonal cuts. This will mean that they have to find areas involving fractions of

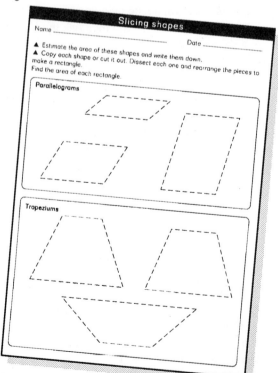

Mass

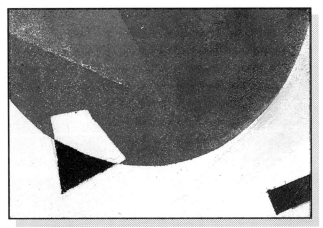

Scientific definitions interpret weight as a force measured in newtons, and mass as the amount of matter in an object, measured in grams and kilograms. In science, mass is used consistently unless a gravitational force is being referred to. We find the mass of an object by using a balance to see how many bricks, grams or kilograms balance with it. When the two sides balance, the masses on either side are equal.

The Earth exerts a gravitational pull on an object. When we jump off a diving board we are pulled towards the Earth by gravity; and if we stand on a ladder the force we exert on the rung is our weight. Our weight depends on gravitational pull, so if we were on the Moon we would weigh less than on the Earth because the Moon's gravitational pull is significantly less than the Earth's. Our mass, however would not change because mass measures the amount of material and this does not change whether we stay on Earth or fly to the Moon.

While it is important that children do not become confused as they learn about mass, many of our everyday phrases are incorrect because they confuse mass and weight. The National Curriculum Mathematics Programme of Study refers to mass but many mathematics schemes talk about weight so there is a dilemma about which word to choose. In practice many talk about weight and leave it to the next stage of education for the distinction to be made. Most of the activities in this chapter use the terminology of mass and those accustomed to working with 'weight' will need to make adjustments accordingly.

SHAPE, SPACE
AND MEASURES

Mass

ORDER THE OBJECTS

To estimate and measure in grams.

†† *Pairs.*

🕐 *30–45 minutes.*

Previous skills/knowledge needed
The children should have been introduced to weighing in grams. They should be able to use a balance to find the mass of objects.

Key background information
The ability to estimate underpins all work in measuring. If children do not have an idea of how a kilogram feels in their hand or a metre looks on the ground any information about the mass or length of an object is going to be relatively meaningless. The ability to estimate grows as children become more familiar with the standard unit that they are learning about. Work on measuring and estimating therefore complement each other, but estimation using a particular unit should not take place until the child has had experience of measuring with that unit and has absorbed how it feels or looks. Many children confuse the size of an object with its mass and it is important that they are given opportunities to correct this misconception through practical activities that encourage them to focus on one measure, in this case, mass.

Preparation
Prepare a set of six objects for the children to estimate and measure the mass. These might be boxes with numbers on the outside, stones of different sizes, toys or a mixture of objects. It is a good idea to include objects which look heavier than they are in order to help the children differentiate between mass and volume. Make a copy of photocopiable page 126 for each child.

Resources needed
Objects to be used for estimating and finding their mass, pan balances, bucket balances, weights, calibrated scales, photocopiable page 126.

What to do
Explain the task on the photocopiable sheet to the children. It is important that they carry out the estimating part of this activity before finding the mass of the objects. They should start by estimating the order of the objects by holding them in their hands and comparing them with each other. The process of comparing six relative estimates is a complicated one and will draw upon the children's skills in using and applying mathematics. Encourage them to work systematically, the position in which they put an object once they have estimated its mass is fairly crucial!

You may want the children to practise using a specific scale or balance or to let them make their own choice about measuring instruments.

Suggestion(s) for extension
The children can investigate the appropriateness of a variety of scales and balances for finding the mass of the objects given. They might want to use bathroom scales, spring balances, digital scales or bucket balances and make judgements about which they would use given a choice. Explain how to set the scales to zero.

**SHAPE, SPACE
AND MEASURES**

Mass

Suggestion(s) for support

Some children may struggle with ordering a relatively large number of objects but be more comfortable with the actual estimating and measuring, so it is important to check on what aspect of the task is causing them difficulty. You can simplify the activity by using fewer objects and by getting the children to estimate the mass of each object and then immediately measure it. Do not use the photocopiable sheet with these children.

If the children have difficulty with estimating and their estimates are very inaccurate they probably need more experience of working with grams so that they gain a better feel for the units. You could encourage them to judge each object against specific masses which are fairly close to the mass of those that they are estimating before estimating the mass of the object.

Assessment opportunities

The written evidence provided by photocopiable page 126 will give you a good insight into the accuracy of the children's estimates but you will need to spend a little time watching them to see how they use the balances or scales. Can they set the balances up if they are not working properly? Do some children assume that the 'largest' objects are also the heaviest? Do they use the scales and balances correctly? Do they make sensible use of the weights or do they add them to the balance in a random fashion? Can the children using the scales read the calibrations correctly?

Display ideas

Make an interactive display using the objects but do not put out the scales and balances initially. Make a chart onto which the children record their estimates of the mass of the objects and when sufficient children have had a go at estimating ask one or two children to find the mass of the objects. Try to find a way to decide whose estimates were the best!

Reference to photocopiable sheet

The children will need photocopiable page 126 to record on as they work. The first column in the table is for writing in the name of the object. The table at the bottom of the page is used for recording the correct order of the objects.

Mass

POTATOES

To estimate and find masses in grams and kilograms.
To convert between metric units of mass. To interpret
scales on measuring instruments.

†† *Pairs.*

⏱ *30–45 minutes.*

Previous skills/knowledge needed
Children should be able to find masses using grams and
kilograms and pan balances. They should be familiar with
decimal fractions and know that a tenth is written as 0.1.

Key background information
Children should be able to make sensible choices about
which measuring instruments to use in particular contexts.
Pressure scales vary in the detail that they offer and children
need to learn to read and interpret the dials. Some scales
are labelled 1kg x 50g which means that the maximum mass
is 1kg and the intervals are 50g. Much of this work is
dependent upon knowledge and understanding of the number
system.

Preparation
Buy (and wash) two kilograms of large potatoes. Make a
copy of photocopiable page 127 for each child.

Resources needed
Calibrated compression scales, more than one type if
possible, potatoes or other large fruit or vegetables,
commercial packages, some showing the mass of the

contents in grams and others as decimal fractions of
kilograms, photocopiable page 127.

What to do
Explain how to record amounts using grams alone or
kilograms alone. Use the packages to help reinforce your
explanation. Check that the children have remembered that
500g is half a kilogram and 250g is a quarter of a kilogram
and that 100g is a tenth of a kilogram. Ask the children to
tell you how they might record a mass of 200 grams as a
decimal fraction of a kilogram. If they struggle with this idea
use 100g masses and a balance to help them see that each
100g is a tenth of a kilogram because it takes ten of them to
balance a kilogram.

Show the children how to record the mass of objects
both as grams and kilograms, for example:

750 grams = 750g = 0.75kg
1200 grams = 1200g = 1.2kg

Demonstrate how to use the scales if the children have
not encountered them before. When children are working
with scales they should be aware that they vary considerably.
The pupils should examine the scale and note the mass
represented by the main interval and each smaller interval
before using them. It is useful to discuss how accurate it is
possible to be using different scales. Sometimes this will be
to the nearest small interval but on some it will be possible
to use half-way between the intervals to obtain a greater
degree of accuracy.

Explain the activity to the children. They should choose
three potatoes, estimate the mass of each and add these to
find the total estimated mass. They then use the scales to

find the actual mass, recording this both as grams and kilograms using the decimal format. They should repeat this twice and find the total mass of all their potatoes, again converting between grams and kilograms. This should mean that they record an amount greater than one kilogram.

Suggestion(s) for extension

Ask the children to investigate various instruments and evaluate their use, discussing their advantages and disadvantages. Digital scales can be included. The children can explain how each one works, draw them, try finding the mass of different objects on each and assess their suitability for working with small and large masses. They can consider the suitability of the various scales for specific tasks such as working out the value of stamps needed for particular packages or letters.

Ask the children to write instructions for reading particular scales accurately (the maximum amount it will record, the value of each interval on the scale, any amounts that can be read between the divisions).

Suggestion(s) for support

Some children may struggle with reading and interpreting the scales. Use amounts such as 500g, 250g, 100g, 50g and put them on different scales, helping them to read the dials. Make sure that the children can count in the intervals displayed on the dials, for example: '50 grams, 100 grams,

150 grams...'. The next step should be to find the mass of unfamiliar amounts. Do not use the photocopiable sheet with these children unless you are sure that the added complication of recording the conversion between metric units will not confuse them.

Assessment opportunities

Can the children find masses using appropriate weights? Are their estimates reasonably accurate? Observe the children as they use the scales. Can they read and interpret the scale? Do they read masses to the nearest interval and can they read half-way between the marks? How accurate is their interpretation?

Opportunities for IT

Older or more able children could use a word processor to write instructions for using a particular set of scales. They should be shown how to set out their work, possibly using formatting commands such as tabs and indents to position text on the page without using the spacebar. If these are printed out in large fonts they can be displayed in the classroom for other children to use.

Reference to photocopiable sheet

The photocopiable sheet provides some examples showing conversions between the metric units to remind the children how to tackle the work and then provides the details of the activity. It is used for recording.

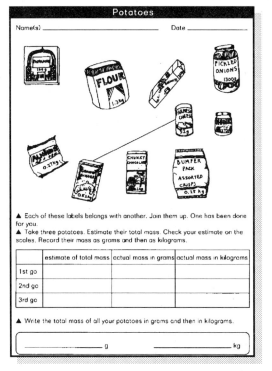

SHAPE, SPACE AND MEASURES

Mass

GOOD BUYS

To calculate using standard units. To solve problems involving mass. To interpret measuring instruments.

†† *Individuals or pairs.*

🕐 *30–45 minutes.*

Previous skills/knowledge needed

Children should be able to use balance scales to find the mass of objects. They should be familiar with the standard units of mass and be able to read and interpret scales. They should be able to calculate using paper and pencil or calculators.

Key background information

The ability to apply their knowledge of mass to real situations is one which is demanded of children by the National Curriculum and by everyday living. The ability to combine number knowledge and understanding with measures is of real importance in making decisions about shopping. This activity is demanding because the children have to find their own ways of answering questions which involve them combining their knowledge of number and measures with finding strategies to solve problems.

Preparation

Bring in the food items listed in 'Resources needed'. Write the cost of each on the packet if these are not present. Make a copy of photocopiable page 128 for each child.

Resources needed

Pressure scales or digital scales, calculators, two packets of biscuits, a box of cereals, one kilogram of fruit – bananas, apples or oranges, photocopiable page 128.

What to do

Talk to the children about the kinds of decisions that adults make when they go shopping. Do they make use of supermarket special offers, buy large packs because they give better value, consult the labels on the shelves which tell them the price of an item of food per 100g? The children may have heard the words but not absorbed their meaning.

Show the children the two packets of biscuits, passing them around the group and ask them to compare them. Help them to find similarities and differences. Be prepared to hear statements such as 'That one's bigger' or 'That one's got more in'. Gradually focus the children's attention on the differences in weight, price, number of biscuits in a packet. Introduce the tasks on the photocopiable sheet and make sure that the children are clear about the meaning of each question.

A maximum of four children at a time will need to work on the activity to ensure that they can all handle the items and use the scales to weigh them if necessary. You may want some children to work on the activity individually whist others will benefit from talking over the strategies with a partner. Some of the questions are deliberately open to interpretation. Encourage the children to find their own way of interpreting the question rather than looking to you for guidance.

SHAPE, SPACE AND MEASURES

Mass

When all the children in the group have completed the activity hold a brief discussion in which you compare their approaches to the questions and get them to explain some of their answers in more detail. Encourage the children to reflect on any gains in understanding by talking about how they could use their strategies next time they are out shopping. They can talk about the number of sweets in a packet, cost, weight and so on although the weights involved are often very small.

Suggestion(s) for extension

Ask the children to investigate gross and net weights of products. The weight of a packet and its contents together is the gross weight; the weight of the contents is the net weight so to find the net weight the children should subtract the weight of the container from the gross weight. Some packages display the gross and net weights while with others it is necessary to empty the contents to find both weights.

Suggestion(s) for support

This activity demands that children use their number skills to solve the problems and some children may struggle to select the correct operation. Those children who struggle can work on one of the questions in more detail, using it as a starting point for further work. For example, they could use a packet of biscuits, work out the cost of one, two, three and so on. If they are unable to tackle the tasks in abstract, encourage them to take out the biscuits and weigh them and then show them how to divide the total weight of the biscuits by the number of biscuits. Encourage them to use this strategy on the next packet.

Assessment opportunities

The written outcomes of the children's work will provide evidence to help you assess their understanding but you may want to watch one or two children more closely as they work. Observe the children as they work and note the strategies that they use to solve the problems. Do they use the scales or solve the problems by calculation? Can they select the appropriate operation? Do they use calculators efficiently and can they interpret the display, rounding as necessary? Do they find certain types of questions more challenging than others? Can they find a way to compare items to decide which is the best buy?

Opportunities for IT

The children could use a spreadsheet to create a table of the results as they work them out. They could then go on to add other items to the chart, for example washing powders. The spreadsheet could automatically work out the price per kilogram, or the number of kilograms per pence by adding formulas into the appropriate cells. The spreadsheet might look something like this:

	a	b	c	d	e
1	Item	weight kg	price pence	price/kg	kg/pence
2	Cleanlt	4.2	345	c2/b2	b2/c2
3	Suds	3.6	296	c3/b3	b3/c3
4	etc..				

The children could use the results to draw graphs of the different items, sorting them from best to worst buy.

SHAPE, SPACE
AND MEASURES

Mass

Display ideas

Make a display of food packages. Ask the children to generate questions for others to answer. These could relate to the number of portions in a box or comparing value for money.

Reference to photocopiable sheet

Photocopiable page 128 provides the task but is not used for recording responses which can be written in books or on paper.

METRIC AND IMPERIAL UNITS OF MASS

To use metric and Imperial measures of mass. To know the approximate metric equivalents of Imperial units.

†† *Small groups.*

🕐 *45 minutes.*

Previous skills/knowledge needed

The children should be able to use standard units of mass. They should be able to estimate and measure using a wide range of standard metric units confidently and accurately. They should be able to use scales or balances to find the mass of objects and quantities. They should be able to use and understand decimal notation in the context of measurement. They should have had some experience of working with the Imperial system.

Key background information

The programme of study for mathematics requires that children should be familiar with both metric and Imperial units of measurement still in daily use, and this knowledge and understanding is listed at Level 5 in the level descriptions for Shape, Space and Measures. Although some Imperial units are becoming less common an understanding of their use is still advantageous in daily life and the relationship between these units and metric ones can be an interesting and challenging area to study, both mathematically and historically. The stone was devised by Edward III in 1351 while metric measures were devised by the French in the eighteenth century. This activity focuses on pounds and ounces and their relationship to grams and kilograms.

Preparation

The children will need to have had some experience in handling Imperial weights so before you tackle the activity make sure that you have talked to them about the Imperial system. Explain that an ounce is generally the smallest unit in use and give the children an opportunity to handle an ounce weight. Tell them that there are 16 ounces in a pound and ask them to work out how many ounces will be in half and a quarter of a pound. Some of the children may be used to buying sweets by the quarter so it is a good idea to remind them about this as some may not realise that the 'quarter'

Mass

is a quarter of a pound. Let the children handle the Imperial weights and lead up to play a blind guessing game in which they guess which of a given set of Imperial weights they are holding.

Fill some opaque bags with quantities of sand, conkers, cubes or fruit.

2 bags containing 1lb

2 bags containing 8oz

2 bags containing 4oz

The paper bags available in supermarkets for carrying and storing mushrooms are ideal for this purpose.

Prepare and display a large chart showing the relationships within Imperial and metric units and display it on the wall a few days before you plan to ask the children to do the activity.

---

1 kilogram = 1000 grams   1 pound = 16 ounces

14 pounds = 1 stone

Abbreviations : lb = pound

oz = ounce or ounces

Resources needed

Bags, fruit, conkers or sand, metric and Imperial weights, scales.

What to do

Tell the children that you want them to find out the mass of each of the bags using Imperial and then metric units. There is no photocopiable sheet for this activity, so the children should find their own method of recording. The children have to work with each of the bags that you have prepared earlier and weigh them using first the Imperial and then metric weights. The children can use pressure scales, digital scales or balances for this activity; you may want them to practise using a particular type of instrument if you need to assess their capability or they can select their own. It is important that all the scales and balances used for this activity are relatively accurate.

If the children find the mass of the 1lb bag first using Imperial and then metric units you could ask them to work out the metric equivalent of half a pound and then a quarter of a pound before using the scales or balances to check. The digital scales will give the greatest degree of accuracy. Encourage the children to make comparisons between the units, such as 'a pound is lighter than a kilogram' as they work.

When the children have finished measuring and converting, hold a brief discussion in which you focus on the similarities and differences between finding masses in both systems. Now would be a good time to remind them about the useful patterns to be found in the metric system. Ask them to work together to make a conversion chart which summarises the results of their work. They may disagree about some of the masses and need to work together to check. As a rough guide, 100g is almost $\frac{1}{4}$lb, 250g is

SHAPE, SPACE AND MEASURES

about $^1/_2$ lb, 500g is a little more than 1lb and 1kg is just over 2lbs. A more specific metric conversion guide is shown below to help you judge the accuracy of the children's findings.

Metric	Imperial
50g	1.8oz
100g	3.5oz
113g	**4oz**
200g	7.0oz
227g	**8oz**
250g	8.8oz
400g	14.2oz
454g	**1lb**
500g	1.1lb
1kg	2.2lb

Suggestion(s) for extension

Ask the children to work out how to convert between metric and Imperial units by calculation. For example, to convert from kilograms to pounds you divide by 2.2 and to convert from pounds to kilograms you multiply by 2.2. Can the children work out how to convert between ounces and grams? They could draw up a conversion chart.

Suggestion(s) for support

Give the children more opportunities to work with the Imperial units before asking them to compare them with those in the metric system. Ask them to make up bags containing specific masses measured using Imperial units.

Assessment opportunities

There will be plenty of opportunities for you to observe the children as they work in order to ascertain whether they have made progress in learning about Imperial units. Can they name the Imperial units of mass in discussion? Do they measure using Imperial units accurately? Are they able to give the rough metric equivalents of pounds and fractions of pounds?

Opportunities for IT

The children could use graphing software to record some of their measurements in both metric and Imperial units and use them to plot a line graph making a simple conversion chart between pounds and kilograms. It may be necessary for children to use similar charts in advance so that they understand how they work. Some children could make different conversion charts in this way, for example ounces to grams, tonnes to tons.

Older or more able children could use a spreadsheet to create an automatic ready reckoner where, as the metric unit is typed in, the Imperial answer is automatically displayed. Children will need to investigate a conversion formula in order to do this either from a table or by weighing a pound weight on a metric scale and using the answer as the conversion constant; for example 1 pound weighs 0.454gm.

	a	b
1	Kilogram	pounds
2	1	a2/0.454
3	2	a3/0.454
4		
5		

Display ideas

Collect some old artefacts, perhaps relating to a history topic, and display them along with a sign asking the children to find their mass using Imperial units. If you can find an old pair of kitchen scales this adds to the authenticity.

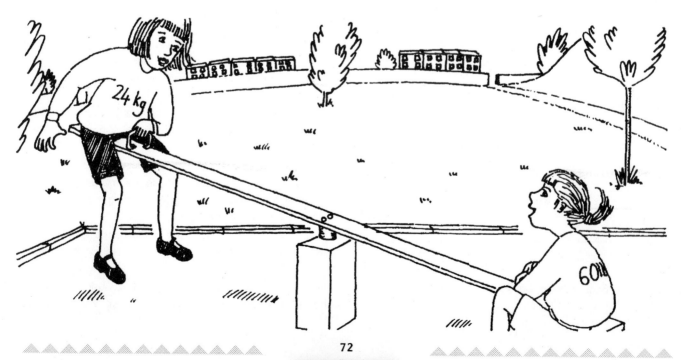

SHAPE, SPACE AND MEASURES

Capacity and volume

Some people are confused about the difference between capacity and volume. The *capacity* of a container is the amount it will hold, such as the number of cornflake packets in a box, matches in a matchbox, sand in a bucket or tea in a mug. The standard metric units of capacity are litres and millilitres; the Imperial units are pints and gallons. The *volume* of an object is the amount of space it occupies. Some containers are hollow so their internal volumes are the same as their capacity. Thicker containers have differing internal and external volumes. The volume of an object is usually measured in cubic centimetres.

The capacity of a container is usually given as the volume of liquid which it will hold. In order to measure both capacity and volume children need an understanding of the conservation of volume. This concept may be more difficult to grasp in relation to liquids than solids because liquids lack a consistent form while the volume of a solid shape can be calculated by constructing it either practically or mentally and counting centimetre cubes. Liquid has to be poured into a measuring container in order to find its volume, and an understanding that the amount of liquid does not vary although it reaches a different height in another container is an important aspect of this measuring process. Children need experience in a variety of contexts, pouring liquid and sand into measuring containers of varying shapes and sizes as they extend their ability to measure by using standard units.

Everyday activities can support the development of children's understanding of capacity and volume.

**SHAPE, SPACE
AND MEASURES**

MYSTERY CONTAINERS

To use 100ml units when measuring capacity. To make and use measuring instruments to estimate and measure the capacity of containers to the nearest 100ml. To read and interpret scales on measuring instruments.

†† *Groups of 4–6 children, children working in pairs within them.*

🕐 *45–60 minutes.*

Previous skills/knowledge needed

Children need to have had experience of measuring the capacity of containers in both millilitres and litres. They should be able to make reasonable estimates when working with litres.

Key background information

None.

Preparation

Make a copy of photocopiable page 129 for each child. Decide whether to use water or sand for the activity. Collect together the containers listed in 'Resources needed' below.

Resources needed

Sand or water, a calibrated litre container, two or three 100ml containers, five unmarked containers (ideally of different shapes, each holding less than a litre and labelled A, B, C, D, E), one unmarked litre container for each pair of children and marker pens to write on them, photocopiable page 129.

What to do

Start with the group together and remind the children of the standard measures they have already experienced. Show them the 100ml mark on a calibrated litre container and demonstrate by pouring from a calibrated 100ml container that ten lots of 100ml are equivalent to one litre. Once this relationship has been established, perhaps by asking different children to experiment, progress to the children making their own measuring instruments in pairs or threes. Provide them with a variety of unmarked litre containers (or if this is not possible let the more able children use larger containers with 100ml calibrations marked) and ask them to use the smaller 100ml container to pour in 100ml of sand or water at a time

and mark off the 100ml divisions. Emphasise the need for accuracy in spacing the divisions when marking off the scale on the outside of their container.

Now that the children have made their own measuring instruments ask them to work together to estimate and then measure the capacity of the five 'mystery containers' marked A, B, C, D and E by using their own containers. Remind

SHAPE, SPACE AND MEASURES

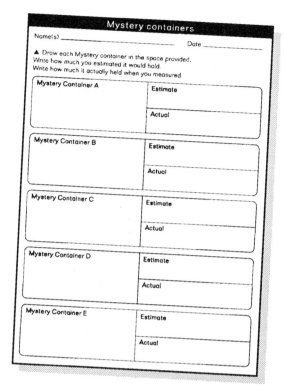

Mystery containers

Name(s) _____ Date _____

▲ Draw each Mystery container in the space provided.
Write how much you estimated it would hold.
Write how much it actually held when you measured.

| Mystery Container A | Estimate |
| | Actual |

| Mystery Container B | Estimate |
| | Actual |

| Mystery Container C | Estimate |
| | Actual |

| Mystery Container D | Estimate |
| | Actual |

| Mystery Container E | Estimate |
| | Actual |

them to estimate first. They should fill a 'mystery container' with sand or water and then pour it into their measuring container and judge the quantity to the nearest 100ml. Allow plenty of time for reading the scales and encourage them to say 'about 200 millilitres' when the amount is not exact or when estimating.

When all pairs have found the capacity of each of the mystery containers ask them to compare their results. Use their recording on the photocopiable sheets to help them see whether their estimates improved during the course of the lesson.

Suggestion(s) for extension
More able children can use smaller containers to make measuring containers with 10ml calibrations. Ask them to find the capacity of smaller containers, for example perfume bottles, shampoo bottles, fizzy drinks cans and fruit juice cartons.

Suggestion(s) for support
Although many children are able to estimate and measure in litres with a fair degree of accuracy some find it more difficult to make sensible estimates of smaller quantities. They need to broaden their understanding of the measures of capacity so that they can make better estimates. By working on the specific quantity of 100ml children should begin to develop a more accurate approach to estimating capacity by building up a mental image of particular units of measure and their relationship to the litre. Since all measurement is approximate it is worth stressing that their first step should be to make a sensible decision about which unit of measure – and therefore instrument – to use for a particular purpose.

You may need to work with some children to ensure that they learn to judge whether the level of the sand or water is closer to, say, 300ml or 400ml as some will automatically read off from the lower mark on the container. If children are having difficulty in estimating it will help if they can see a given quantity, so ask them to fill the 100ml container to help them.

Assessment opportunities
Observe the children as they fill the containers and check whether they can make reasonable estimates before measuring. When they pour sand or water into their calibrated measuring container do they use the scale correctly? Can they read off the scale to the nearest 100ml?

Display ideas
The children could make a display of containers which hold the same amount as the mystery containers, setting a challenge to others to find the container which holds the same as, for example, Mystery Container B.

Reference to photocopiable sheet
Photocopiable page 129 is an aid for recording measurements in the course of the practical task. The children draw the mystery container and then record their estimate and the actual capacity of each container. The children's recording can be used to support further discussion as they compare results at the end of the activity.

HOW MUCH DOES IT HOLD?

To make reasonable estimates of the capacity of containers. To use measuring instruments to measure in litres and millilitres.

†† *Children work in pairs after initial input from teacher.*

🕑 *45 minutes.*

Previous skills/knowledge needed
Children need to have had experience of measuring the capacity of containers in both millilitres and litres. They should be able to make reasonable estimates when working with these standard measures. The ability to picture mentally certain amounts and to compare the amount being estimated with a mental image should have been developed through activities such as 'Mystery Containers' which provide practice in working with specific quantities.

Key background information
Regular practical work develops the ability to estimate how much is held by containers of varying shapes and sizes. As children extend their knowledge of the standard units of

SHAPE, SPACE AND MEASURES

measure for finding the capacity of containers by using litres and millilitres separately they need to learn to combine the two. As they will be working with quantities over a litre their estimations may be less accurate than when working with smaller quantities.

Preparation

During the course of work on capacity set up a capacity table which holds calibrated measuring containers, sand and a variety of containers which hold more than a litre but with their capacities covered up. You may want to label them A, B, C, D, E, F, etc.

Copy photocopiable page 130 for each child.

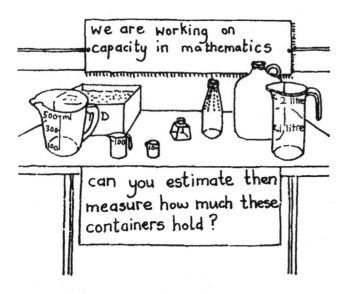

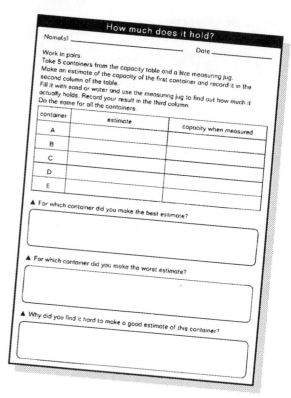

Resources needed

Litre measuring jugs or containers calibrated in 100ml divisions, sand or water, a variety of containers holding more than a litre, photocopiable page 130.

What to do

Work on the first part of the activity with a large group and then let the children work on the section involving estimating and measuring in pairs to suit your timetable. Choose a large container with a capacity of more than one litre and ask the group what they would use to find out how much it will hold. Encourage the use of the correct language: capacity, litres, millilitres. During the course of the discussion you will probably want to highlight the need for the children to make a rough estimate of the amount that it will hold so that they can use an appropriate measuring container to find the capacity. You could ask questions like: 'Shall we use this 100ml measuring jug?' 'Why not?' 'Do you think it holds more than a litre?'

Once there is broad agreement over which measuring jug to use, fill the container with your chosen material (sand, water) and demonstrate how to pour it into the litre jug, filling it to the litre mark if there is sufficient sand or water and reading off the scale when part of a litre remains.

Ask the children to work in pairs to estimate and measure the capacity of five containers. They can use the photocopiable sheet to record on. When all the children have completed the activity hold a discussion with the whole group about how they made their estimates, which containers held most and least and the effect of the shape of a bottle on their perception of its size.

Suggestion(s) for extension

Ask the children to make a container that holds at least a litre using sugar paper and then encourage them to get their friends to estimate and measure its capacity.

Suggestion(s) for support

Work closely with the children as they estimate, encouraging them to measure a litre first and then think about how much is left.

Assessment opportunities

Note the strategies the children use when estimating and measuring. Can they make reasonable estimates? Does their recording show that their estimates have improved as they worked on the activity? Can they use the scale on the measuring jug accurately?

Display ideas

Children could produce a poster called 'Estimating Tips' showing useful hints for improving estimates.

Reference to photocopiable sheet

The photocopiable sheet provides a format on to which children can record their findings. It gives little information about how to tackle the task, giving them an opportunity to use and apply their knowledge. You may wish to check whether the children have found the difference between the estimate and the actual measure for each container in order to be able to identify their best and worst estimates. You will probably want the children to record their measurements using *l* and *ml*, for example 1l and 300ml.

⬛ FIND THE VOLUME

To find volumes by counting cubes. To develop understanding of the need for a formula for the volume of a cuboid (v = l × b × h).

✝✝ *Large group then pairs and individuals.*

🕐 *45–60 minutes.*

Previous skills/knowledge needed

Children should be able to build cubes and cuboids with smaller cubes.

Preparation

Build a cube out of 1cm cubes with dimensions 4 × 4 × 4. Build a cuboid with dimensions 6 × 2 × 2. Make copies of photocopiable page 131 for each child and page 132 for those needing support.

Resources needed

1cm interlocking cubes, wrapping paper for extension activity, sticky tape, photocopiable pages 131 and 132.

What to do

Explain that you will be working on finding the volumes of models. Remind the group that the volume is the amount of space that a shape takes up.

Use the cube first. Tell the children that you are going to give them just a glimpse of it and then ask them to estimate how many cubes were used to make it. Hold up the cube for about five seconds then hide it. Ask the children to turn to a neighbour and talk about how many cubes they think were needed to make it. Move around the class as they talk and if they simply say a number to each other encourage them to justify their estimates by asking questions like: 'Why do you think 20?' 'Could it be more? ... Why not?' 'Jasmine thinks 40, could she be closer?'

After two minutes stop the discussion between the children and work with the whole group again. Ask for a number of estimates and write them on the blackboard. Tell them that you need to find out which is right.

Ask some children to explain how they had come to their figure. Show them the cube briefly again and ask them to close their eyes and picture it before trying to work out how many small cubes are within it. Ask for some second estimates before showing them the cube. This time count the cubes together, perhaps using a child to help. Stress the idea of finding out how many cubes in a layer and counting the number of layers.

If anyone uses the idea of multiplying the number of cubes in a layer by the total number of layers let them explain it to the rest of the group. You will probably need to clarify some of the explanations. Do not worry if some children do not use this idea initially. As they work on subsequent activities they will begin to develop an understanding of the volume of a cuboid as *v = l × b × h* (length times breadth times height).

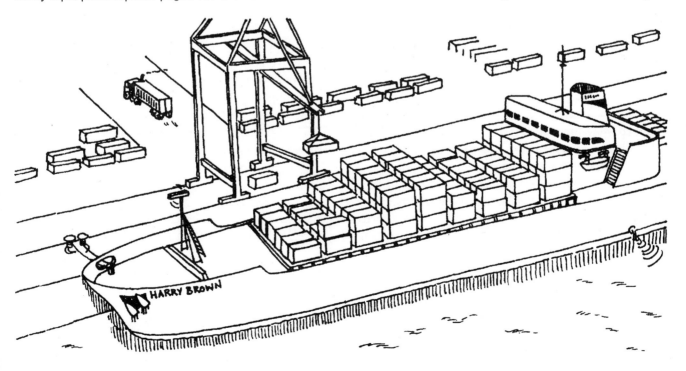

SHAPE, SPACE AND MEASURES

Repeat the process with the cuboid. This time encourage the children to focus on the number of layers as they visualise the model. Show them how to record the volume as 24cm³.

Ask the children to work in pairs, building cubes and cuboids and counting the number of cubes in each model for about ten minutes. As the children work, help them to use the formula $v = l \times b \times h$ informally by encouraging them to look at slices or layers within the model. Beware of teaching this formula to children whose conceptual grasp of volume is weak. Use the photocopiable sheets for recording.

Suggestion(s) for extension

Ask the children to construct from wrapping paper the net of a cube or cuboid to hold one of the models. When they have wrapped a number of models they can swap models with each other and calculate their volumes, using rulers to measure and calculate dimensions using the formula $v = l \times b \times h$.

Suggestion(s) for support

Some children will need to take a model apart and count the cubes individually. Children will differ in the way that they visualise the number of cubes in a shape. Some may build up the layers from the bottom horizontally whilst others may visualise slices from the top. If children are finding it difficult to count, show them how to take the models apart both ways and choose the one which feels most natural to them. Show them a 3 × 3 layer, ask them to tell you how long, how wide and how high it is and how many cubes there are altogether. Add another 3 × 3 layer, and another, recording the number in each layer and the total number each time. Photocopiable page 132 can be used as an alternative to photocopiable page 131 with children who require support.

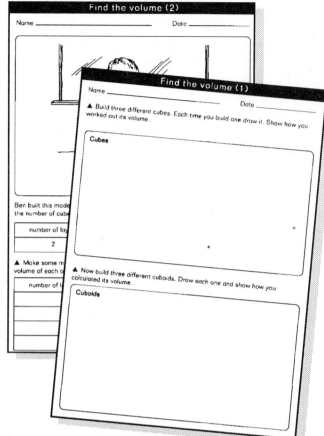

Assessment opportunities

Observe the children as they work. Have they developed a system for counting the number of cubes in a model? Do the children count each cube to find the volume of a model? Can they use their knowledge of multiplication to calculate the number of cubes in a layer? Can they use the formula $v = l \times b \times h$?

Opportunities for IT

Children could use this work to investigate how cubed numbers grow. They could use the results from the practical work with graphing software to create block or line graphs of the growth of the number of cubes in a particular shape.

Alternatively the children could create a simple spreadsheet on which they plot the results and then use a formula to extend these further. They might compare surface area with volume to see if there is a relationship.

The spreadsheet might look something like this for a cuboid:

	b	c	d	f	g
1	height	width	length	Volume	surface area
2	1	1	1	b2xc2xd2	2(b2xc2)+4(c2xd2)
3	2	2	2	b3xc3xd3	2(b3xc3)+4(b3xd3)
4					

Children can then use the spreadsheet to model different cuboids to see the effect in the surface area of changing the length. The results from the spreadsheet can also be plotted on a bar or line graph. By replicating the formulas down the spreadsheet it is easy for children to see how the volume of a cube grows very quickly. The results can also be displayed as a graph using the data in the spreadsheet.

Display ideas

Make a display of some of the models that the children have built. Get them to design labels showing the volume of these models and set the challenge to match the labels to the models within a specific time limit.

Reference to photocopiable sheets

Photocopiable page 131 is designed to be open-ended to enable children to show how they calculated the volume of each of their models. It can be customised to give specific models for the children to build, draw and find the volume of, for example by writing: 'Build models with these dimensions: $3 \times 4 \times 4$, $4 \times 3 \times 3$, draw each one and explain how you worked out its volume.'

Photocopiable page 132 provides a more structured approach for children needing further support, giving children practice in counting each layer at a time and finding the total number of cubes used by adding the number in each layer.

PINTS AND LITRES

To know Imperial units of capacity and their approximate metric equivalents.

†† *Large group and individuals.*

◔ *30–40 minutes.*

Previous skills/knowledge needed

The children should be able to estimate and measure using standard units of litre and ml. They should be able to read scales to measure quantities of liquid. They should understand simple common fractions.

Key background information

Knowledge of the relationship between Imperial and metric units of measurement are required while we live in a society in which many purchases and measurements are still made using Imperial units. There is no obvious relationship between pints and litres and it is therefore important that children have opportunities to work on practical activities to develop an intuitive feel for the connection between them.

Preparation

Collect together the containers listed in 'Resources needed'. Make a copy of photocopiable page 133 for each child.

Resources needed

Calibrated litre container, pint bottles or mugs, litre container, photocopiable page 133.

What to do

Discuss with the children how milk and petrol are bought, how recipes are written and the words that adults use when they talk about them. They are likely to mention that adults use the words pints, gallons and possibly fluid ounces. Explain why these words are less common nowadays.

Concentrate on the relationship between litres and pints. Hold up a pint of water and a litre of water and ask which is the larger quantity – the litre or the pint. Ask for suggestions as to how to find out which is more. Ideas may include pouring the contents of one bottle into another, measuring each in a calibrated measuring container or weighing the contents of each bottle.

Set the group the task of finding out which is the larger unit of measure in small groups. Encourage the children to work co-operatively in deciding how to tackle the task.

When the children have completed this part of the activity, discovering that a litre is more than a pint, demonstrate that a pint is just over half of a litre (570ml) by pouring the contents of the pint bottle into a litre measuring container and discussing what fraction of the container is full. Ask the children to estimate how many millilitres are equivalent to the pint and then look at the scale to check.

You can show that a litre is equivalent to $1^3/_4$ or 1.75 pints by pouring liquid from the litre container into pint

SHAPE, SPACE AND MEASURES

Opportunities for IT

The children could use graphing software to record some of their measurements in both metric and Imperial units and use them to plot a line graph making a simple conversion chart between pints and litres. It may be necessary for children to use similar charts in advance so that they understand how they work.

Older or more able children could use a spreadsheet to create an automatic ready reckoner where, as the metric unit is typed into the spreadsheet, the Imperial answer is displayed. Children will need to investigate a conversion formula in order to do this either from a table or by measuring accurately how many litres there are in a pint and using the answer as the conversion constant; for example 1 litre equals 1.75 pints.

	a	b
	Litres	Pints
1	Litres	Pints
2	1	a2 x 1.75
3	2	a3 x 1.75
4		
5		

Display ideas

Children could make a collection of containers whose capacity is measured in Imperial and metric units, for example milk cartons, kitchen jugs.

Reference to photocopiable sheet

Photocopiable page 133 provides a summary of the facts the children will have learned during the lesson. It gives a structure for the work that the children will tackle mainly unaided by the teacher.

containers if you wish. If you judge that this is not appropriate for the group then omit this part of the activity and amend photocopiable page 133 by deleting the final question.

Ask the children to work in groups, repeating the process of comparing pints with litres using the measuring jugs and answering the questions on the photocopiable sheet individually. Visit the groups as they work, noting any difficulties they may be having.

Suggestion(s) for extension

Ask the children to work out how to use calculators to convert pints to litres and litres to pints. It will help to study a conversion table – cookery books are a good source of these. Ask the children to devise a conversion scale or ready reckoner to convert between metric and Imperial units.

Suggestion(s) for support

Omit the comparison between litres and pints made by pouring from the litre to the pint container. Amend photocopiable page 133 so that the final question is not tackled by the children.

Assessment opportunities

Observe the children as they work and as they complete photocopiable page 133. Do they understand the relationship between pints and litres?

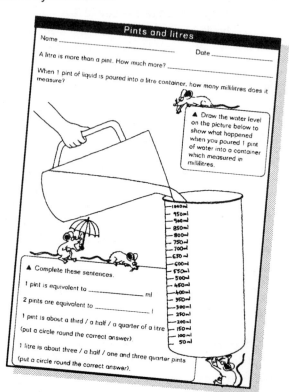

Pints and litres

Name _____

Date _____

A litre is more than a pint. How much more? _____

When 1 pint of liquid is poured into a litre container, how many millilitres does it measure?

▲ Draw the water level on the picture below to show what happened when you poured 1 pint of water into a container which measured in millilitres.

▲ Complete these sentences.

1 pint is equivalent to _____ ml

2 pints are equivalent to _____ l

1 pint is about a third / a half / a quarter of a litre (put a circle round the correct answer).

1 litre is about three / a half / one and three quarter pints (put a circle round the correct answer).

SHAPE, SPACE AND MEASURES

Time

Time is a difficult measure for children to learn about because there is nothing concrete for them to touch or compare. Young children learn that time is continuous by experiencing activities in which they measure the passing of time using non-standard units and then move on to learn how to read the dials on clocks which use the standard units (seconds, minutes and hours).

It is a good idea to use digital and analogue clocks alongside each other so that children learn about the format which is becoming more and more common in their everyday lives. Many children find it easier to tell the time using the digital format because there are fewer mathematical ideas involved. When we tell the time using an analogue clock, an interval between two numbers can be five minutes or an hour and we need to understand the idea of 'past' and 'to' and be able to use fractions as well. A hand pointing at 3 has to be interpreted as fifteen or three or quarter past! The child who has trouble using a traditional clock-face may have problems in differentiating between left and right and so confuse 9 and 3 or quarter past and quarter to, confuse the hour hand with the minute hand (after all, an hour is longer than a minute) or be unable to count in fives.

A child can tell the time without having a concept of time. Telling the time is a matter of learning to read the dials. It is important that older children continue to work on timing activities that help them to learn about the duration of time intervals alongside work on telling the time.

SHAPE, SPACE
AND MEASURES

Time

WHAT'S THE TIME?

To tell the time to the nearest minute. To use and interpret digital and analogue clocks and record times.

†† *Group, pairs and individuals.*

🕐 *First part 30 minutes, second part 30–40 minutes.*

Previous skills/knowledge needed

The children should be able to tell the time, probably to five minute intervals and certainly using half past, quarter past, quarter to. They should be able to count in fives.

Key background information

This activity can be tackled in two parts. The first part works on telling the time in one minute intervals up to 'half past' and is fairly straightforward. The second part deals with times between half past and the hour and is more demanding.

Preparation

Make a copy of photocopiable page 134 for each child. Photocopy some of the TV pages if there are not enough for children to be able to share one between two.

Resources needed

Digital and analogue clock-faces, several TV pages from newspapers or previous week's TV guides, photocopiable page 134.

What to do

First part

Ensure that the children remember that there are sixty minutes in an hour before you start. Set the analogue clock to show 9.23 and demonstrate that to read the time it is necessary to count around in five-minute intervals from 12 and then forward in one minute intervals until the minute hand is reached. Show a number of different times which involve fewer than thirty minutes and encourage the children to help you find out the time, for example: 'eight twenty-five ... sixteen minutes past eleven ... seven minutes past two ...'.

Distribute the analogue clock-faces, call out some times and get the children to show those times on the clock. Vary the way in which you say the time so that they get used to the different forms. No recording should take place here as the purpose of the activity is to help the children get used to reading and showing times. As they work on these times show them the equivalent one using the digital clock-face and draw their attention to the fact that the hour is always read before the minutes, for example: 'three oh seven'.

Finish this part of the activity by asking the children to suggest times for their partner to show on the clock-face. They can record these times using clock stamp pads in their books and writing the times in words underneath. Make sure that they write the time shown both ways: '6.10 or ten past six'.

Second part

Work on times where there are more than thirty minutes involved. Show the children 3.40 on the clock-face and say the time both as 'three-forty' and 'twenty to four'. Ask them to show the same time on their clocks and then explain that they should count on in five-minute intervals until they get to 12 (the beginning of the hour). It is important that the children understand that by doing this they are saying how many more minutes there will be until the next hour is reached. You will probably need to take this part slowly as there are a number of ideas for the children to absorb. You may need to remind the

---

What's the time?

Name _____ Date _____

▲ Choose six TV programmes and find out what time they start. Record them on this table.

	name of programme	starting time
1		
2		
3		
4		
5		
6		

Programme Name

7.35 or twenty five minutes to eight

▲ Show the time on the clocks then write the times underneath.

Programme 1
Programme 2
Programme 3
Programme 4
Programme 5
Programme 6

SHAPE, SPACE AND MEASURES

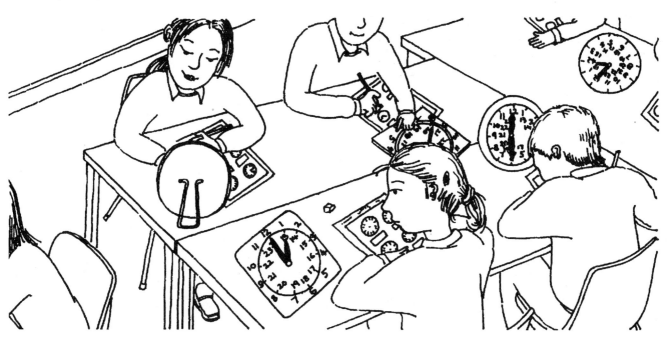

children that they only need to count on in five-minute intervals to the end of the hour if the minute hand is showing more than 30 minutes. It is a good idea to start by showing them times such as 7.35, 7.40, 7.45, 7.50 and 7.55 so that they begin to be able to recognise these by sight and form a mental image which will help them to approximate times later.

Move on to more difficult times such as 11.43 gradually. You may find that some children find it easier to start at 12 and count back to the minute hand in five-minute intervals, dealing with the left over minutes at the end. Ensure that the children can translate between digital and analogue clocks. The children can work in pairs, saying a time for their partner to show and then checking it together.

Finally distribute the TV pages from the newspapers. The children take a day's television and record the starting times of six programmes using photocopiable page 134. They show the time on the clock-faces and write it in two different ways underneath.

Suggestion(s) for extension

Ask the children to calculate the length of their six TV programmes. They will probably find it easier to do this using counting-on methods than performing a conventional calculation.

Suggestion(s) for support

It is harder to record a time or set a clock to a certain time than it is to say or read a time from a watch or clock so work closely with the children when they tackle this aspect of the activity.

It is a good idea to use a digital clock first as it is easier to tell the time using these. Make sure that the children are not struggling because they are unable to count fluently in fives. Frequent reinforcement is essential for those children whose ability to tell the time is insecure.

Assessment opportunities

Observe the children as they work, and check their recordings using photocopiable page 134. Can they tell the time using analogue clocks to the nearest minute? Can they relate digital and analogue times to each other? Can they show a time written in the TV guide on an analogue clock-face?

Opportunities for IT

There is a wide array of specific software aimed at helping children to tell the time and teachers need to select software which is appropriate for their children's age and attainment. Framework software with several different options, like *My World 2* with the *Telling the Time* file or Topologika's *Talking Clocks* are particularly useful as activities can be selected to support particular difficulties or interests.

An extension activity, which tackles issues within the control technology area of IT, might be to get children to programme a video recorder using information from a list of television programmes. They could word process a set of instructions for others to use.

Display ideas

Ask the children to make a poster by cutting out pictures of digital and analogue clock-faces and using collage techniques. You could challenge them to choose three items from the poster and record them in the alternative format.

Reference to photocopiable sheet

Photocopiable page 134 asks children to record times similar to those worked on in both parts of the activity. It is best completed after the children have done the second part rather than in two stages. The children should record the starting times of the TV programmes as they are written in the newspaper.

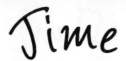 Time

HOW LONG DOES IT TAKE?

To use stopwatches to time events to the nearest tenth and hundredth of a second. To read and interpret displays on stopwatches.

†† *Large group then pairs.*

🕐 *45–60 minutes.*

Previous skills/knowledge needed

Children should have an understanding of decimal place value to two decimal places.

Key background information

An understanding of the passing of time is as important as the ability to tell the time and children need to gain a feel for the length of certain intervals. The ability to time events to a fair degree of accuracy is particularly important during scientific investigations and in sport and there will be many cross-curricular opportunities for the children to use this knowledge and understanding.

Preparation

None needed.

Resources needed

Digital and analogue stopwatches and watches.

What to do

Show the children the various timing devices and demonstrate their use. Remind them that a minute is divided into 60 seconds and explain that breaking each second up into tenths and hundredths of a second gives a greater degree of accuracy. Discuss situations where there is a need for such accuracy, for example in athletics and swimming meetings. It is a good idea to start a stopwatch and get the children to count the seconds out loud as the hand goes around so that they begin to experience how long the intervals are.

'Time' a minute mentally. The children hide their eyes and you tell them when to start timing, pressing a stopwatch at the same time. You tell them when a minute is up. Repeat this a few times and then let the children work with partners, taking it in turns to time a minute. As the children work on

this activity visit the pairs and make sure that they can read the stopwatches. Move on from giving them experience of a minute to get them to estimate a minute – one child estimates and the other operates the stopwatch. Help them to read the dials, making sure that they are as accurate as possible. After they have had two or three turns, ask the children to change stopwatches with another pair so that they work with a different form of measuring instrument. They should teach the other pair how to read the dials on the stopwatch they have just handed over.

Next ask each pair how long they think it will take you to write your name (neatly) 20 times on the board or on a large piece of sugar paper. The children could record their estimates or you could write a few of them on the board. It is a good idea to get the children to time you doing the writing and it is useful if they all do this using their stopwatches as they will have practice in reading the dials. Carry out the task and discuss the accuracy of their estimates with the children. Ask the children to estimate and then time how long it takes them to write their names ten times and then five times. Does the time taken halve?

The children should now be able to suggest events which they could estimate and time around the classroom or in the playground if this is appropriate. These might include balancing bricks on top of each other, drinking a glass of water through a straw, saying a multiplication table three times. Encourage them to record both their estimate and the time taken.

Suggestion(s) for extension

Some children may like to investigate the effects of practice on the time taken to carry out a task. They can repeat the same task several times, recording the time taken each time and noting any differences. A graph can be used to display the data.

Suggestion(s) for support

Some children may be confused by the fact that there are sixty seconds in a minute but that seconds are then broken down into tenths and hundredths. A place-value board divided into minutes, seconds, tenths of seconds and hundredths of seconds can be used to record times.

SHAPE, SPACE AND MEASURES

Assessment opportunities

When you carry out the first part of the activity observe how sensible are the children's estimates of the time taken to write your name on the board. Do they estimate in seconds, in minutes, or in a combination of the two? As the children work in pairs observe whether their estimates improve as they work on the activity. Note whether they use the decimal system correctly when timing the events. Can they work out how much time has elapsed using an analogue watch with a second-hand or with a digital watch? Can they time an event to the nearest second, tenth or hundredth of a second using a stopwatch?

Opportunities for IT

Children could use timing devices attached to a computer through a suitable control box and use it to time events, particularly those of a short duration such as reaction times. This could be set up to work when children turn on or off a switch or press a button. More sophisticated control situations could be organised with older or more able children to record time after one event and to stop recording after another event, for example when a marble starts to go down a ramp and when it reaches the bottom.

Children can also set up monitoring devices, such as a temperature probe in cooling water and allow the computer to plot temperatures at set intervals and plot a cooling curve as it happens. This is a useful activity for helping children to understand the passage of time and the way that the graph varies over time. Monitoring over longer periods could also be organised, for example, plotting temperatures throughout the night.

MY TV WEEK

To calculate with 12-hour times.

†† *Individuals.*

🕐 *30 minutes.*

Previous skills/knowledge needed

Children should be able to tell the time confidently. They should be able to add and subtract.

Key background information

Calculating with time is an important part of our daily lives. In order to add and subtract times children have to use a number system based on the fact that there are 60 minutes in an hour.

Preparation

Ask children to bring in the previous week's TV guide from home. Copy photocopiable page 135 for each child.

Resources needed

TV guides, clocks or clock-faces, photocopiable page 135.

What to do

Ask the children to practise counting around an analogue clock-face in five-minute intervals. Ask them if they can work out how long it is from, say, 6.25 to 7.10 and then practise with a few different times, encouraging the children to count on in sensible intervals. Give the children some clues about your favourite TV programme. These should help the children to focus on the categories of programmes on photocopiable

SHAPE, SPACE AND MEASURES

page 135. Give clues such as : 'It's on BBC1 on a Monday and Thursday. It starts at 7.30 pm and finishes at 8.00 pm and lasts for 30 minutes. It's a soap opera.' The children should use their TV guides to help them work out your mystery programme. Ask them to work in pairs to make up some clues for each other before showing them photocopiable page 135 and explaining the task.

The children should use the TV guides to work out how much time they spend each week watching programmes in each of the categories listed. They may need to use clock-faces to help, but encourage the use of mental methods to work out the length of the programmes if at all possible. Elicit the fact from the children that there are 60 minutes in an hour in order to help them make accurate calculations or they may find the difference between the finish and start times by doing a straightforward calculation using base 10.

Suggestion(s) for extension
Children can construct a bar chart or a line graph showing their TV watching habits. They could work out the average time they spend watching TV.

Suggestions for support
Work closely with the children and help them to find a method of recording the times. They may well need help with working out the length of the programmes and a clock with moveable hands would be useful. They should count on in five- or ten-minute intervals as they move the hands from the start time to the finish time. They can take one day's viewing and use the start and finish times to calculate how much time they spend watching TV on one day or they could order programmes according to their duration.

Assessment opportunities
The photocopiable sheet will provide evidence of the children's ability to calculate with time.

Opportunities for IT
Children could use a graphing package to plot and display their viewing habits for the week. Alternatively, a simple database could be set up with a record for each child with their total viewing for each day of the week:

Name	Mitesh
sex	male
age	10
Monday	3 hours
Tuesday	3.5 hours
etc	
Total	15.5 hours

The information could be sorted or searched and questions framed and answered such as:
Who watches the most TV in a week?
Do boys watch more than girls?
Which is the most popular night for watching TV?
Children could also use the graphing facilities to plot graphs and pie charts about watching habits, by day or by individual pupils.

Display ideas
Make a photomontage using pictures and extracts from TV guides and surround it with statements from the children's work about the time spent watching the different programme categories.

Time

Reference to photocopiable sheet

The sheet is used to calculate and record the time spent watching programmes in each category; the categories can be changed to suit the interests of the children. It does not provide a format for children to use so they will need to think carefully about how they use it. The children should show their working and try to present their results as clearly as possible. They could use the back of the sheet to summarise their findings or draw a graph.

24-HOUR TIME LINE

To order events using 12-hour clock and 24-hour clock times and understand the relationship between the 12- and 24-hour systems.

†† *Large or small groups initially and then individuals.*

🕐 *45 minutes.*

Previous skills/knowledge needed

Pupils will need to be able to tell the time using analogue clocks.

Key background information

Familiarisation with 24-hour clock times is important before further work on timetables is tackled. The digits after the hour on a digital display are minutes past the hour, so 12.40 can be explained as forty minutes past 12.

Preparation

Draw a 24-hour time line on a large sheet of paper.

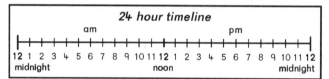

Resources needed

An analogue clock-face showing 12- and 24-hour times, paper, pencils, rulers and colouring pencils.

SHAPE, SPACE
AND MEASURES

Time

What to do

Explain that in the 24-hour system four digits are used to show the time. The first two show the hours and the last two the minutes. Use the clock-face to demonstrate how the 24-hour system works by counting around the clock starting at 1 and going on to 12, then 13, 14, 15 and so on. Ask the children to join in and repeat this a few times, counting both forwards and backwards. When the children have become familiar with the counting, highlight equivalent times by stopping at, say 15.00 and asking what the equivalent 12-hour time is. Encourage the children to spot the rule for converting a 24-hour time to a 12-hour time by subtracting twelve hours from the 24-hour time. The children may need to practise saying 24-hour clock times as 'fourteen hundred hours'.

The children may have seen digital clocks displaying times in a variety of ways, for example: 15.00 or 1500. Encourage them to tell you about these and discuss with them the various places in which they have seen digital displays.

When you judge that the children have understood the principle, show them your prepared timeline and ask them to tell you what they notice. Discuss the reasons for 'midnight' appearing at both ends of the line. Introduce the children's individual task by asking them to draw out their own timeline and mark equal divisions on it to show a whole day. They should show both 12- and 24-hour times on it. When they have completed the timeline they can illustrate it by drawing lines to specific times and showing what they do at those times. So, for example, if a child has chosen to illustrate a school day they might draw themselves leaving the house at 08.30, doing PE at 11.00, eating lunch at 12.30, playing at 13.00, having the register taken at 13.15 and so on.

When all the children have finished their timelines it is useful to ask them to compare them. They can ask each other questions about their work, for example: 'What do I do at 13.00?', 'How do you say 2 o'clock in the afternoon as a 24-hour clock time?'

Suggestion(s) for extension

Children can make a chart showing events and their times using both systems.

Event	Time using the 12 hour system	Time using the 24 hour system
Get up	7.45 am	0745 hours
Have breakfast	8.00 am	0800 hours
Catch bus	8.22 am	0822 hours

Suggestion(s) for support

Some children will find it challenging to draw out their own timeline but they should be encouraged to persevere. The hardest part is marking the divisions and it is a good idea to get them to draw a line of a length which is easy to mark out into 24 divisions. You may even want to provide a half-finished line for these children. It is important to check that they have begun to label their divisions correctly.

Assessment opportunities

Note the children's responses as they work on the first part of the activity. Can they convert a 24-hour system time to a 12-hour one? Do they count easily from 12.00 to 13.00? Do their timelines demonstrate that they can order events?

Display ideas

The timelines can be displayed together on the wall.

SHAPE, SPACE AND MEASURES

Assessment

The National Curriculum demands that teachers' own professional judgement play a greater role than ever in informing teaching and learning. Assessment retains a central role in the Mathematics curriculum. Effective assessment in mathematics, as in any curriculum area, plays a crucial role in good teaching and learning because it helps to identify strengths and weaknesses and provides valuable information to enable teachers to plan appropriate work for children.

Most of the activities in this book highlight formative assessment opportunities related to the particular task. The activities in this chapter are generally intended to assess more than one learning objective and should support the teacher in making assessments of children's learning in relation to aspects of the National Curriculum Programme of Study.

The assessment activities range from specific closed tasks which demand a narrow range of responses to more open-ended investigative tasks. When children work on such tasks it is important that the teacher spends time in observing the children as they work. Each assessment activity has a teachers' recording sheet which highlights the main assessment objectives and gives guidance on what to look for and how to interpret the outcomes of children's work.

Where possible, information is given to help teachers judge the National Curriculum level of the mathematics in the activity to support summative assessments which are made at the end of a key stage. It is important to remember that a level can only be given when judging a child's performance in all the components of an attainment target.

SHAPE, SPACE
AND MEASURES

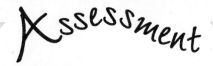

THREE-DIMENSIONAL SHAPE

To name three-dimensional shapes, recognising their geometrical features and properties. To make three-dimensional shapes. To recognise the reflective symmetries of three-dimensional shapes.

†† *Groups of 3–6 children.*

⏰ *10 minutes for first activity; 10–20 minutes for second activity depending on child's ability.*

Key background information

The children can do both parts of this assessment orally and practically. If you want to do this you will need to set aside time to spend on observing the children. The activities will help make judgements about the children's understanding of the properties of three-dimensional shapes as well as their ability to make and construct.

At Level 3 children should be able to classify three-dimensional shapes in various ways using mathematical properties. At Level 4 they should be able to make three-dimensional models by linking given faces or edges. At Level 5 they should be able to construct models, measuring and drawing angles to the nearest degree.

Preparation

Make copies of photocopiable sheets 137, 138, 139 and 140. Each child will need a copy of sheet 137 if you are going to assess their knowledge of properties through their writing. The other sheets can be used for reference or construction by some children, so you will probably need fewer of these. You may wish to photocopy page 136 which is an optional sheet to aid teachers when recording outcomes of pupils' assessment. Collect together the equipment listed in 'Resources needed'.

Resources needed

A set of three-dimensional shapes including cubes, cuboids, tetrahedra, other pyramids for example, square-based, sphere, cone, cylinder, triangular prism (include environmental shapes such as commercial packages), Polydron or Clixi, squared paper, plain paper, rulers, protractors, scissors, glue, sticky tape, photocopiable pages 137, 138, 139, 140 and 136 if required.

What to do

Decide whether to do this part of the assessment orally or using photocopiable page 137. Provide the group with the three-dimensional shapes and hold a brief discussion with the children, asking them to point out similarities and differences between the shapes. This should enable you to make an initial assessment of the children's use of the mathematical terminology relating to shape should you wish to assess this aspect of 'Using and Applying' mathematics. Ask the children to describe cubes, cuboids, spheres and pyramids including their properties on photocopiable page 137. Encourage them to write about the number and shape of the faces, edges, vertices and symmetries of the shapes. Ask them to bring you their completed sheet when they have

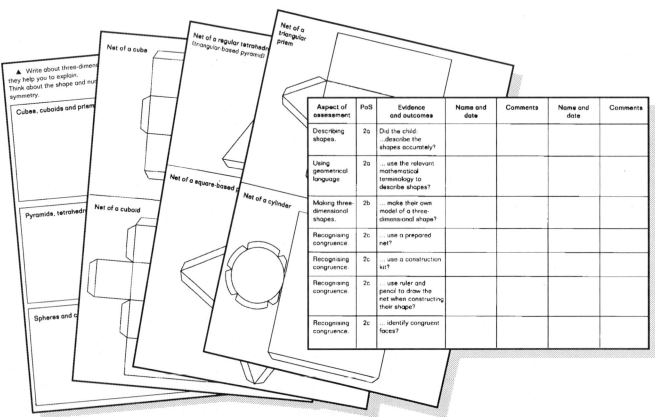

SHAPE, SPACE AND MEASURES

finished and use this opportunity to clarify anything they have written down, you might want to ask specific questions to help them confirm your judgements. The following list of the properties of three-dimensional shapes is for teachers' reference:

cuboid	six rectangular faces, opposite faces congruent (the same shape and size), twelve edges, eight vertices
cube	six congruent square faces, twelve edges, eight vertices
sphere	one curved face, no edges or vertices
cylinder	three faces: two parallel congruent end faces, joined by one curved face, two curved edges, no vertices
pyramid	any polygon as a base, all other faces triangles which meet at a point
tetrahedron	pyramid with four congruent equilateral triangular faces, twelve edges and six vertices
cone	a pyramid with two faces: one circular base and the other curved, one curved edge, one vertex (or apex)
prism	three-dimensional shape which can be cut into congruent sections identical in shape to the two parallel end faces

Once they have completed the first part of the assessment ask the children to choose one of the three-dimensional shapes from photocopiable sheets 138, 139 and 140 and make their own model of it using any materials they choose.

Explain that you would like them to work as accurately as possible and that they should try to make their model as close to the actual size as they can. It is more challenging to construct the net of a three-dimensional shape alone than from a given net or a commercial construction kit such as Clixi or Polydron.

Reference to photocopiable sheets
Photocopiable page 137 is used for children to record their knowledge about the properties of three-dimensional shapes. Photocopiable pages 138, 139 and 140 provide nets of the common three-dimensional shapes for children to use as reference or in the course of their constructions. The photocopiable teachers' recording sheet 136 provides some guidance on what to look for and how to interpret the outcomes when assessing individual children.

TWO-DIMENSIONAL SHAPE

To recognise the geometrical properties of two-dimensional shapes. To recognise the reflective and rotational symmetries of two-dimensional shapes. To understand the congruence of simple shapes.

†† *Children working individually within groups.*

🕐 *20–40 minutes depending on child's ability.*

Key background information
The assessment activities which follow can only provide information on specific aspects of two-dimensional shape. When making assessments of children's understanding in this part of the Mathematics curriculum it is most important that teachers consider work from a number of sources in order to build up a true picture. The first part of this activity can be done orally. You are likely to elicit more information from the children if you choose to carry out the activity this

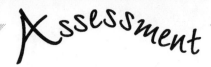Assessment

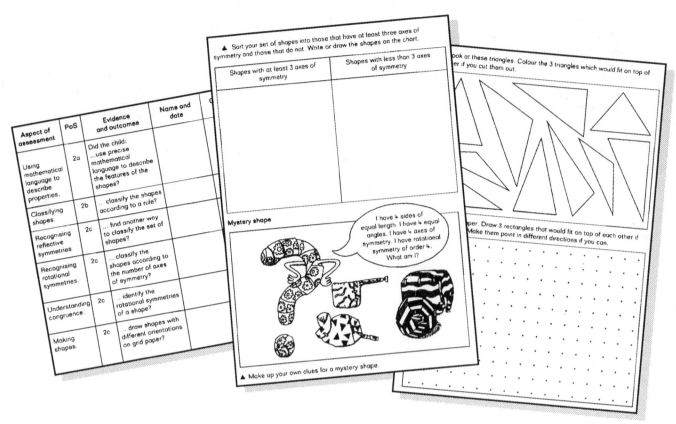

way but it is more time-consuming. You may want to work orally with those children whose writing ability lags behind their mathematical understanding or those who are less likely to show their true understanding when confronted with a photocopiable sheet.

At Level 3 children should be able to classify shapes in various ways using their mathematical properties which may include reflective symmetry. At Level 4 they should be able to draw common shapes in different orientations on grids and identify those shapes which are congruent. They should be able to identify the orders of rotational symmetry of two-dimensional shapes. At Level 5 they should be able to use angles when constructing shapes and know all the symmetries of two-dimensional shapes.

Preparation
Copy photocopiable page 142 for each child and also photocopiable page 143 if you decide to use it. You may wish to photocopy page 141 which is an optional sheet to aid teachers when recording outcomes of pupils' assessment. Collect together the equipment listed in 'Resources needed'.

Resources needed
A set of two-dimensional shapes including squares, rectangles, different triangles, pentagons, hexagons, octagons, decagons, different quadrilaterals, (for example, trapezia, parallelograms, rhombi), rulers, protractors or angle measurers, set squares, photocopiable pages 142 and 143, and 141 if required.

What to do
Decide whether to carry out the first part of the activity orally or using the photocopiable sheet. Using a set of shapes for each group of children, hold a brief discussion about the properties of the shapes to remind them of key words such as sides, corners, parallel, perpendicular, angles, axes of symmetry, rotational symmetry. If the group is to work on paper explain what they have to do on the photocopiable sheets. Encourage them to use the shapes as they work as some may think that they have to do the work mentally. Spend a short time with each child after they have completed the sheet discussing the reasons for their sorting. Can they demonstrate why a shape is classified as having less than three axes of symmetry?

If you are carrying out the assessment orally, start by asking each child to sort the shapes into two sets – one having at least three axes of symmetry and one having two or less. When the children have done this ask them to find a different way of sorting the shapes. You will need to note whether the children sort accurately as there will be no written evidence for you to evaluate subsequently.

The second part of the assessment has to be carried out using the photocopiable sheet. Explain the tasks to the children before they start. If the children are familiar with the term 'congruent' then remind them of it before they start the task. Some children may want to make replica triangles and fit them on to each other to test for congruence, others may measure the length of sides and size of angles using rulers and protractors or angle measurers, others may be able to visualise. Encourage them to find ways of solving the

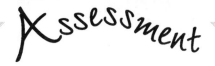

problem themselves. Can the children explain why they have identified particular shapes as congruent? Can they tell you any other similarities or differences between the shapes on the sheet?

Reference to photocopiable sheets

Photocopiable sheets 142 and 143 provide the context and format for recording this assessment. The use of photocopiable page 142 is optional. The photocopiable teachers' recording sheet 141 provides some guidance on what to look for and how to interpret the outcomes when assessing individual children.

POSITION AND MOVEMENT

To transform two-dimensional shapes by translation, reflection and rotation, creating, visualising and describing patterns.

✝✝ *Children working individually within a group of 4–6.*

🕐 *15–40 minutes depending on child's ability.*

Key background information

The movement of shapes is a dynamic process and one which should not be assessed solely through written activity as some children may demonstrate their understanding in other contexts more successfully. It is important, therefore, to consider evidence gained from previous work in mathematics and teacher observation when making judgements about children's abilities in this area. All the instructions for this activity can be given verbally if children need more support. Some aspects of this activity are challenging for children. If

their finished patterns have some minor mistakes within them you may still judge that they understand translation, reflection or rotation.

Children should be able to reflect simple shapes in mirror lines to achieve Level 4 and use language associated with angle, measuring and drawing them to the nearest degree at Level 5.

Preparation

Make copies of photocopiable pages 145 and 146 for each child. You may wish to photocopy page 144 which is an optional sheet to aid teachers when recording outcomes of pupils' assessment. Use cubes to make a square-shaped pattern (shown below) which has reflective and rotational symmetry.

Resources needed

Mirrors, colouring pencils, rulers, interlocking cubes, photocopiable pages 145 and 146 and 144 if required.

What to do

Start by showing the children your square-shaped pattern made from cubes. Ask them to tell you what they notice about it. Can they use the terms symmetrical and/or rotational symmetry? Do they identify all the axes of symmetry?

Ask a child to make a shape the same as the one on photocopiable page 145 by joining cubes. Demonstrate that the shape can move in different ways. Can the children

SHAPE, SPACE
AND MEASURES

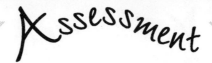

Assessment

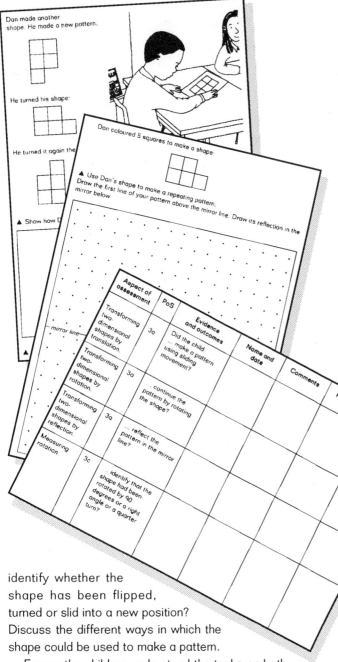

LENGTH, AREA AND MASS

To understand and use the language of measures. To make estimates with appropriate units of length, area and mass. To choose and use appropriate instruments for measuring length and mass. To find areas by counting and other methods.

†† *Small group of three children working individually.*

🕐 *30–45 minutes depending on child's ability.*

Key background information

This activity is open-ended. It is designed to let children make decisions about their mathematics whilst giving the teacher opportunities to assess knowledge, skills and understanding in length, area and mass. It can also address many of the elements contained in the Attainment Target 'Using and Applying' mathematics. This activity assumes that the children are accustomed to working with the mathematical terminology of mass. If this is not the case you will need to alter photocopiable page 149 so that the language makes the task accessible to the children.

At Level 3 children should be able to use non-standard and standard units of length and mass in a variety of contexts. At Level 4 they should be able to make choices and use appropriate measuring instruments for length and mass, find perimeters and find areas by counting squares. At Level 5 they should be able to make sensible estimates, convert between metric units and know the rough metric equivalents of Imperial units.

Preparation

Collect together about six boxes. The boxes should be of different sizes ranging from a cereal packet down to a small stock cube box or matchbox.

Fill five of them with a variety of materials, so one might contain dried peas, another polystyrene chips, another Plasticine, another a stone, another a lump of wood and so on. They should all have a different mass. Put something heavy in one of the smaller boxes and leave the largest box empty. Cover the boxes with paper and label them A, B, C, D, E and F.

Make copies of photocopiable page 149 for each child. You may wish to photocopy pages 147 and 148 which are optional sheets to aid teachers when recording outcomes of pupils' assessment.

identify whether the shape has been flipped, turned or slid into a new position? Discuss the different ways in which the shape could be used to make a pattern.

Ensure the children understand the tasks on both photocopiable sheets. Some children may wish to use cubes or other apparatus to help them transform the shapes. When the children have completed the task ask them to use cubes or colour squares to design their own pattern with diagonal axis symmetry. This will ensure that the children will have worked on reflecting patterns in horizontal and diagonal mirror lines. This is more challenging than reflecting a shape about a vertical axis of symmetry.

Reference to photocopiable sheets

Photocopiable pages 145 and 146 provide the context for the activity and a means for structuring the recording of the children's work. The photocopiable teachers' recording sheet 144 provides some guidance on what to look for and how to interpret the outcomes when assessing individual children.

Resources needed

Six boxes, wrapping or plain coloured paper, sticky tape, materials for filling boxes, pan scales, a set of weights up to and including 1kg, rulers, a transparent grid marked in 1cm squares, photocopiable page 149, and 147 and 148 if required.

SHAPE, SPACE AND MEASURES

What to do

Give the group the set of parcels, provide each child with the photocopiable sheet and explain to them that you want them to find out as much as they can about the parcels. Tell them that you want them to show you how much they know about length, area and mass so they should concentrate on these measures. Explain that you need to know how well they can estimate before they start, give each child a parcel and ask them to estimate the length of one of its edges, the area of one of its faces and its mass. Get them to tell you first and then record on the sheets afterwards. This will give you an opportunity to question each child who gives an incorrect answer. Once this part of the assessment is complete you might want to leave the group to work unaided, but will need to return whenever you can to observe the children as they work.

When the children have finished they will need to have an opportunity to discuss their results with you. You may want

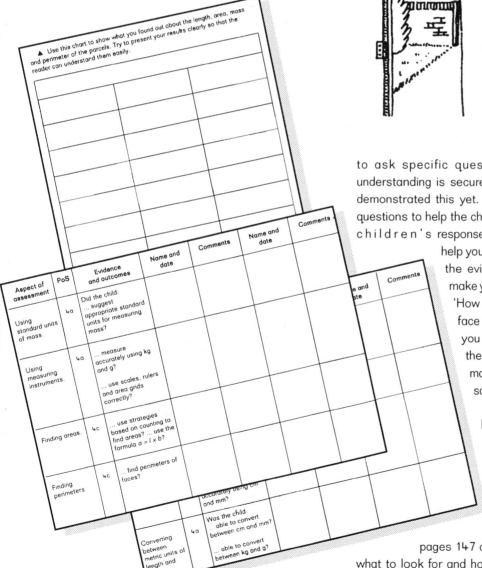

to ask specific questions to assess whether their understanding is secure in certain areas if they have not demonstrated this yet. You may need to ask more open questions to help the children structure their approach. The children's responses on the photocopiable sheet should help you formulate questions by highlighting the evidence that is needed to help you make your judgements. Ask questions like: 'How long is the shortest edge?' 'Which face did you find the area of?' 'How did you find its area?' 'Which parcel weighs the heaviest?' 'What is the combined mass of these three parcels?' 'Can you say that in kilograms and grams?'

Reference to photocopiable sheets

Photocopiable page 149 is used to record the children's findings about the dimensions, area and mass of the parcels. The photocopiable teachers' recording pages 147 and 148 provide some guidance on what to look for and how to interpret the outcomes when assessing individual children.

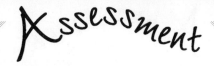

CAPACITY AND VOLUME

To understand and use the language of measures. To make sensible estimates with appropriate standard units of capacity. To choose and use appropriate instruments for measuring capacity. To read scales accurately. To understand the relationship between units of capacity. To find volumes by counting methods.

✝ *Small groups of 2 or 3 children, working individually.*

🕐 *15–30 minutes for each part depending on child's ability.*

Key background information

This activity is practical and should enable teachers to assess children's skills, knowledge and understanding of volume and capacity through a combination of observation, questioning and considering written outcomes. It is possible to assess some of the aspects of the Attainment Target 'Using and Applying' through this activity. It is designed to assess the understanding of children who are able to use standard measures.

The activity is in two parts, the first assesses the children's understanding of capacity and the second, their understanding of volume. The activities can be carried out separately. It is more difficult to estimate volume and capacity accurately than other measures so do not expect the children to be as proficient at estimating as they are in, say, length. At Level 3 children should be able to use non-standard and standard metric units of capacity. This activity assesses the ability to use standard units of capacity. At Level 4 they should be able to suggest that the contents of a jar will be measured in millilitres (and possibly litres depending on its size) and measure reasonably accurately, using the scale on the outside of the measuring container. They should be

able to use counting methods to find volumes. At Level 5 they should be able to convert between metric units of capacity and make sensible estimates.

Preparation

Set up a measuring table holding capacity measuring equipment and containers. Make copies of photocopiable pages 151 and 152 for each child. You may wish to photocopy page 150 which is an optional sheet to aid teachers when recording outcomes of pupils' assessment.

Resources needed

A number of coffee jars or similar containers of different proportions, calibrated measuring cylinders/jugs, materials for measuring, for example rice, sand, water, scissors, centimetre cubes, photocopiable pages 151 (for assessing capacity) and 152 (for assessing volume) and 150 if required.

What to do

Provide each child with photocopiable page 151 and their own set of three containers, two of which should hold more than 500ml. Explain that you would like them to put the containers in order of capacity according to their own estimates first, and then find out how much each container holds, measuring as accurately as possible and recording their new order. Tell them that they will need to write down what they have found out. You will need to observe the children as they begin the activity and visit them from time to time as they work in order to evaluate how accurately they measure and estimate. If children are unable to measure using units they may choose to compare the containers by pouring from one to another.

Once they have found the capacity of all three of their containers they should choose two of the containers and

SHAPE, SPACE AND MEASURES

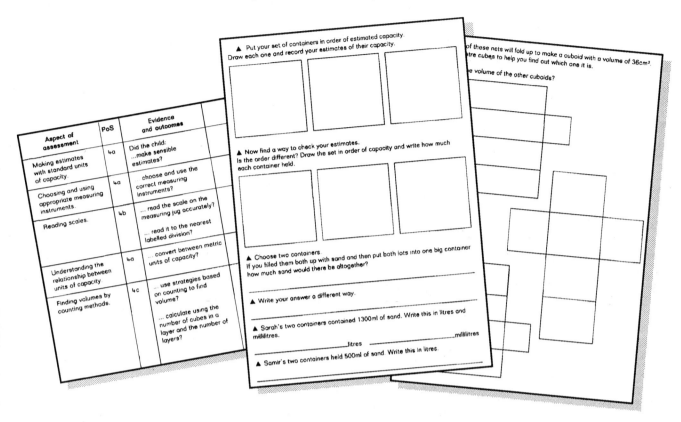

work out how much rice/sand/water there is when the contents are combined and record the answer on their sheet. Some may choose to carry out a calculation, adding the contents of the two containers together, others may need to use the measuring equipment again. The approach taken is not significant as this part of the activity aims to assess whether the child can convert between litres and millilitres. So if the total was 1300ml then the child should be able to record it as 1 litre 300ml or 1.3 litres.

When the children have finished the activity spend about two minutes with each one, discussing their answers. Encourage them to explain how they came to their answers. If they have trouble finding a way to express the combined amount of two containers, prompt them by asking questions like: 'What if you said it as litres and millilitres?' 'Can you say it in decimal form?'

In order to assess the children's understanding of volume give them each a copy of photocopiable page 152 and ask them to cut out each net and find out which resulting cuboid has a volume of 36cm³.

They may approach the problem in different ways, some may try to make model cuboids with a volume of 36cm³ before cutting out the sheet and then find that they do not fit. As you observe the approaches the children take you may feel able to assess them against some of the elements of 'Using and Applying'. Remember that you are assessing how they find the volumes of the models, can they use simple counting methods, or are they working at a higher level multiplying the number of cubes in each layer by the number of layers or even using the formula $v = l \times b \times h$?

Reference to photocopiable sheets

Photocopiable page 151 provides the context and evidence for the capacity assessment. Photocopiable page 152 provides the context for the volume assessment and nets which the children cut out. The photocopiable teachers' recording sheet 150 provides some guidance on what to look for and how to interpret the outcomes when assessing individual children.

TIME

To use the language of time. To measure time using clocks and stopwatches. To tell the time using digital and analogue clocks.

†† *Children working in groups of 4–6 for first part of activity. Children working individually within a large group for second part of the activity.*

🕐 *15–30 minutes, depending on the child's ability.*

Key background information

This activity is designed to provide a format for teachers to assess the two main aspects of time taught at primary level: measuring the passing of time, and telling the time including the use of the 24-hour clock.

At Level 3 children should be able to use non-standard and standard units of time in a range of contexts. At Level 4 they should be able to choose and use appropriate units and instruments for measuring time, interpreting them with appropriate accuracy.

up, ask them to demonstrate their marble run, taking turns to time the marble's journey using the stopwatch. Observe each child as they use the stopwatch in order to assess their ability to use it.

For the second part of the assessment you will need an analogue clock-face. Tell the children four different times and ask them to record those times as you say them on the first four analogue clock-faces on photocopiable page 154. Tell them that the first two times are morning times and the second two are afternoon times. They should then record these times using the 24-hour clock format on the digital clock-faces underneath. Then say three times using the 24-hour clock format and ask them to record them in analogue form using the last three clock-faces on the sheet.

Reference to photocopiable sheets

Photocopiable page 154 is used to record the children's responses to the teacher's questions. The photocopiable teachers' recording sheet 153 provides some guidance on what to look for and how to interpret the outcomes when assessing individual children.

Preparation

Copy photocopiable page 154 for each child. You may wish to photocopy page 153 which is an optional sheet to aid teachers when recording outcomes of pupils' assessment. Collect together the equipment listed in 'Resources needed'.

Resources needed

A large analogue clock-face, a stopwatch, six rulers, a large board, a large lump of Plasticine, four cubes and a marble, photocopiable pages 154 and 153 (if required).

What to do

The first part of the activity is carried out by children working in groups. It assesses the ability to time events using a stopwatch. It is therefore not suitable for children who have been timing events using non-standard units. The second part of the activity can be carried out with a large number of children as it relies upon the teacher asking questions to which children respond individually on their copies of photocopiable page 154.

Give a group of children a board, marble and a lump of Plasticine. Tell them that they have to use the materials to make the marble run. The marble has to travel from one end of the board to the other, taking as long as possible. Give the group ten minutes in which to complete the task. When the time limit is

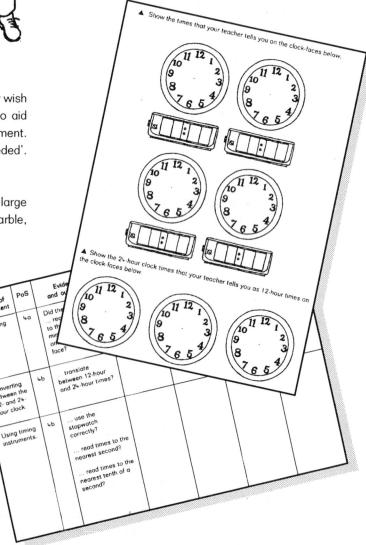

98

Photocopiables

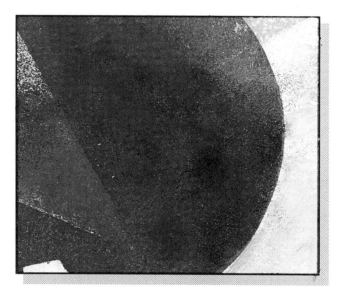

The pages in this section can be photocopied for use in the classroom or school which has purchased this book, and do not need to be declared in any return in respect of any photocopying licence.

They comprise a varied selection of both pupil and teacher resources, including pupil worksheets, resource material and record sheets to be completed by the teacher or children. Most of the photocopiable pages are related to individual activities in the book; the name of the activity is indicated at the top of the sheet, together with a page reference indicating where the lesson plan for that activity can be found.

Individual pages are discussed in detail within each lesson plan, accompanied by ideas for adaptation where appropriate – of course, each sheet can be adapted to suit your own needs and those of your class. Sheets can also be coloured, laminated, mounted on to card, enlarged and so on where appropriate.

Pupil worksheets and record sheets have spaces provided for children's names and for noting the date on which each sheet was used. This means that, if so required, they can be included easily within any pupil assessment portfolio.

Photocopiable sheets 136 to 154 are to be used for the purposes of summative assessment and accompany the activities in the Assessment chapter.

Cubes (1)

Name _____   Date _____

The net of a cube is made by joining 6 squares. There are 11 different nets of a cube.

▲ Which arrangements of 6 squares fold to make cubes? Can you find all 11?
▲ Draw different arrangements of 6 squares and then test them out. Mark the arrangements that are nets of cubes with a tick or colour them in.

I found _____ different nets of a cube.

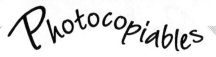

Cubes (2)

Name _____   Date _____

▲ Colour the squares on this net so that it will fold up to make a cube exactly the same as the one that you have been shown by your teacher.

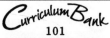

**SHAPE, SPACE
AND MEASURES**

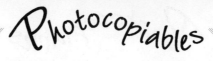

Prisms, see page 17

Prisms

Name(s) _____   Date _____

▲ Draw the net for a triangular prism and make it. It must be 8cm long and the triangular faces should have sides that are 4cm long.

▲ Can you draw the net for a different sort of prism and make it?

SHAPE, SPACE AND MEASURES

Sorting three-dimensional shapes, see page 19

Sorting three-dimensional shapes (1)

Name _____   Date _____

▲ Write the names of the shapes in the correct regions of these Venn diagrams.

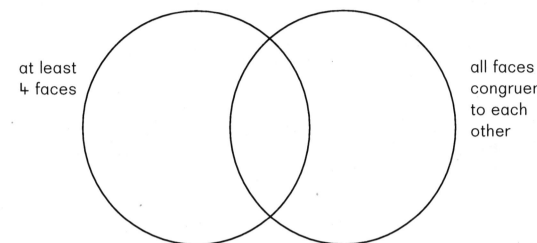

at least 4 faces

all faces congruent to each other

prisms

five faces

▲ How have these shapes been sorted? Label the sets.

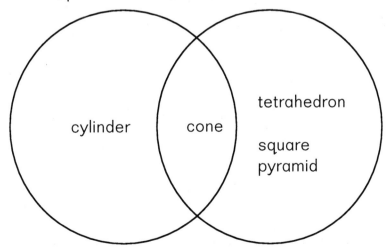

cylinder   cone   tetrahedron

square pyramid

SHAPE, SPACE AND MEASURES

Sorting three-dimensional shapes (2)

Name(s) _____   Date _____

Some useful words to use when describing three-dimensional shapes.

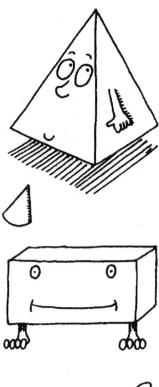

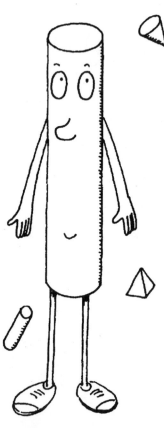

Face

Edge

Vertex

Vertices

Base

Regular

Equal

Flat

Curved

Straight

Right Angle

Equilateral

Square

Triangular

Circular

Rectangular

Hexagon

Pentagon

Prism

**SHAPE, SPACE
AND MEASURES**

Symmetries of three-dimensional shapes

Name _____   Date _____

▲ How many planes of symmetry do each of these shapes have?

a _____   b _____   c _____

▲ Use cubes.

▲ Make a shape that has *one* plane of symmetry.

▲ Make a shape that has *two* planes of symmetry.

▲ Make a shape that has *four* planes of symmetry.

▲ Can you make a shape that has *no* planes of symmetry?

SHAPE, SPACE AND MEASURES

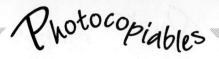
Spots and nets

Name _____   Date _____

▲ Join 4 cubes. How many different shapes can you make by joining 4 cubes?
Draw them on isometric dotty paper. An example is shown below.

▲ Choose two of your shapes. Look at the drawings you have done. Can you
make the nets for two of your 4-cube shapes? Pick an easy one first.

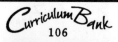
SHAPE, SPACE
AND MEASURES

Fold and count, see page 26

Fold and count

Name _____ Date _____

▲ Use a rectangular piece of paper. Fold it once. How many sides has the new shape? What is it called?

The shape made by folding here is an irregular hexagon. It has 6 sides.

▲ What other shapes can be made by folding a rectangle *once*?

Can you make:

a different rectangle	a hexagon	an octagon
a pentagon	a heptagon (7 sides)	a nonagon (9 sides)?

▲ Make a display to show other people how you made your new shapes.

▲ Try starting with a square, a triangle or a regular hexagon. What different shapes can you make?

SHAPE, SPACE AND MEASURES

Two cuts, see page 27

Two cuts

Name _____   Date _____

▲ Using two cuts on a square, what shapes can you make?
▲ Record your work.

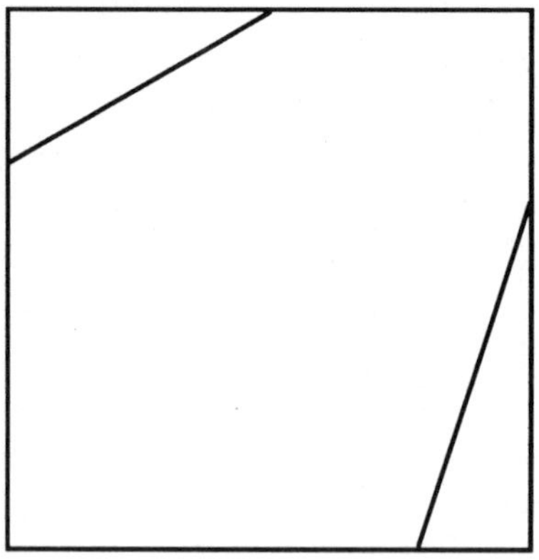

1 hexagon
2 right-angled triangles

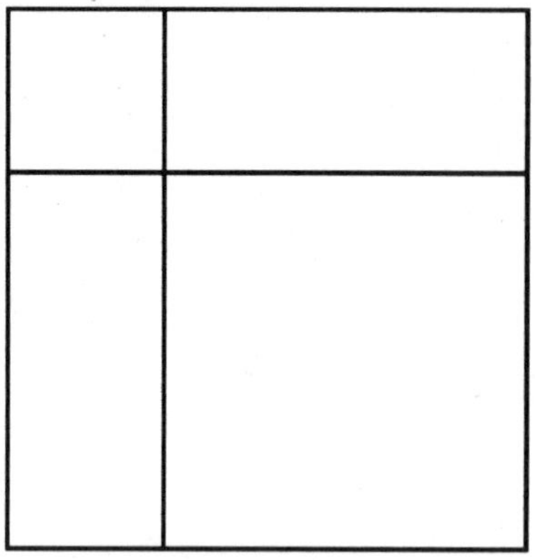

2 squares
2 rectangles

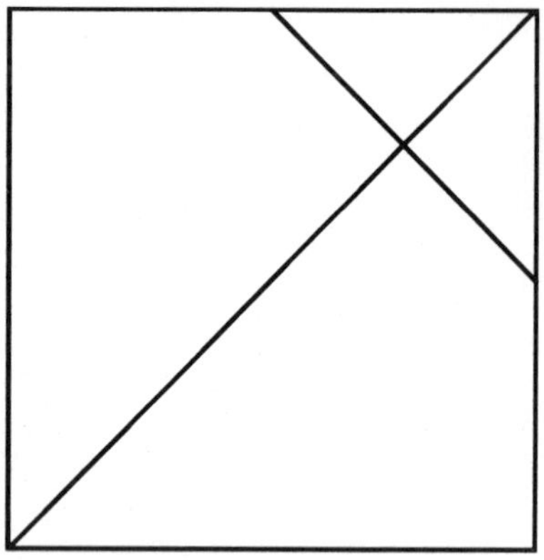

2 quadrilaterals
2 isosceles triangles

SHAPE, SPACE
AND MEASURES

Find the shape, see page 28

Find the shape

Name _____ Date _____

Congruent shapes are exactly the same shape and size but they might be in different positions.

▲ Find the pairs of congruent shapes. Draw a line to join them.

SHAPE, SPACE AND MEASURES

Triangles, see page 30

Triangles

Name _____ Date _____

▲ Join the corner of each shape to all its other corners.
▲ Look for triangles.
▲ Colour equilateral triangles yellow.
▲ Colour isosceles triangles blue.
▲ Colour scalene triangles orange.

SHAPE, SPACE
AND MEASURES

Quadrilaterals, see page 31

Quadrilaterals

Name _____   Date _____

▲ Test some quadrilaterals for their symmetries.
▲ Record your results on the chart.

	Number of lines of symmetry	Order of rotational symmetry
Parallelogram		
Rectangle		
Rhombus		
Square		
Trapezium		

▲ Why do you think that squares and rectangles have a different number of lines of symmetry?
▲ Why do you think that squares and rectangles have a different order of rotational symmetry?

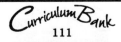
SHAPE, SPACE AND MEASURES

Turning and shrinking shapes, see page 33

Turning and shrinking shapes

Name _____   Date _____

▲ Draw a regular shape accurately. Find the midpoint of each side. Join the points. Continue.

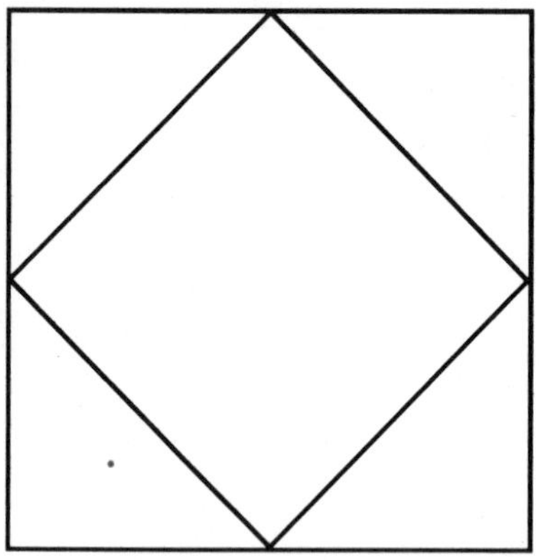

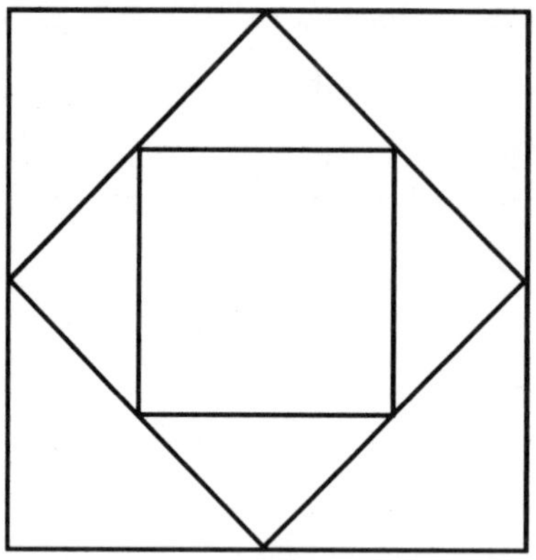

▲ Try making a shrinking shape pattern by starting with a triangle or a rectangle.

▲ What happens if you join points that are not midpoints? Try it. Make sure that each point is the same distance from one corner.

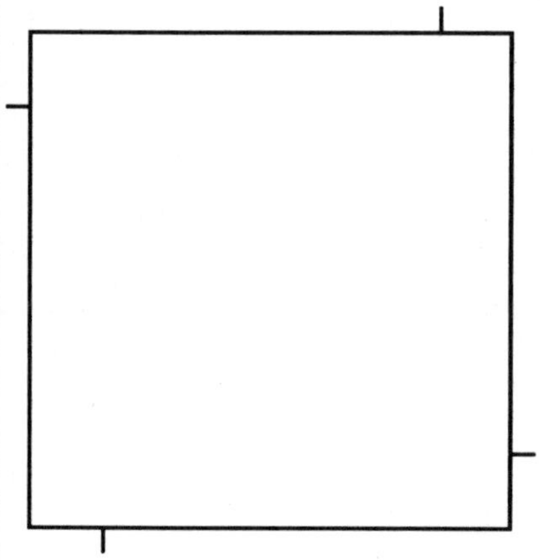

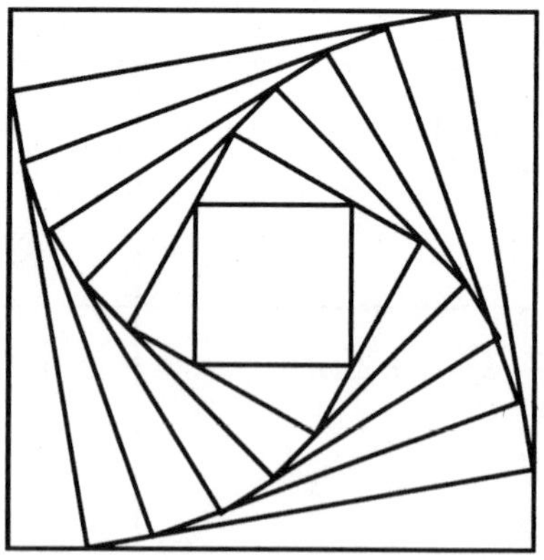

▲ Try with different shapes.

SHAPE, SPACE
AND MEASURES

Pieces, see page 37

Pieces

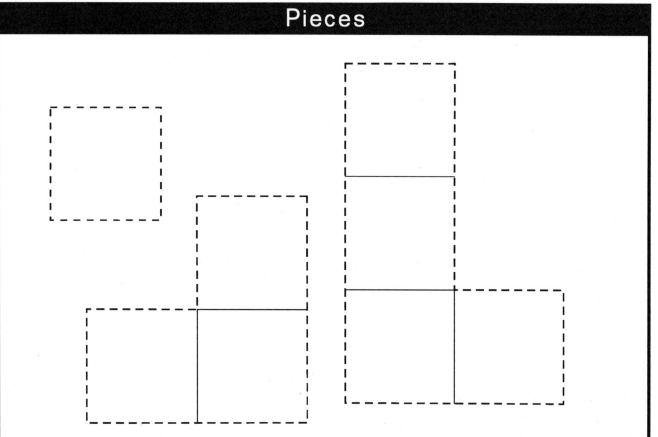

The pieces above have been cut out and arranged to make a shape with one axis of symmetry (see below).

▲ Cut out the pieces above and use them to make as many different shapes as possible with reflective symmetry.

▲ Do any have two axes of symmetry?

axis of symmetry

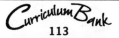

SHAPE, SPACE AND MEASURES

Shapes and mirrors, see page 39

Shapes and mirrors

Name _____ Date _____

▲ Complete the reflections. Use a mirror to help if you want.

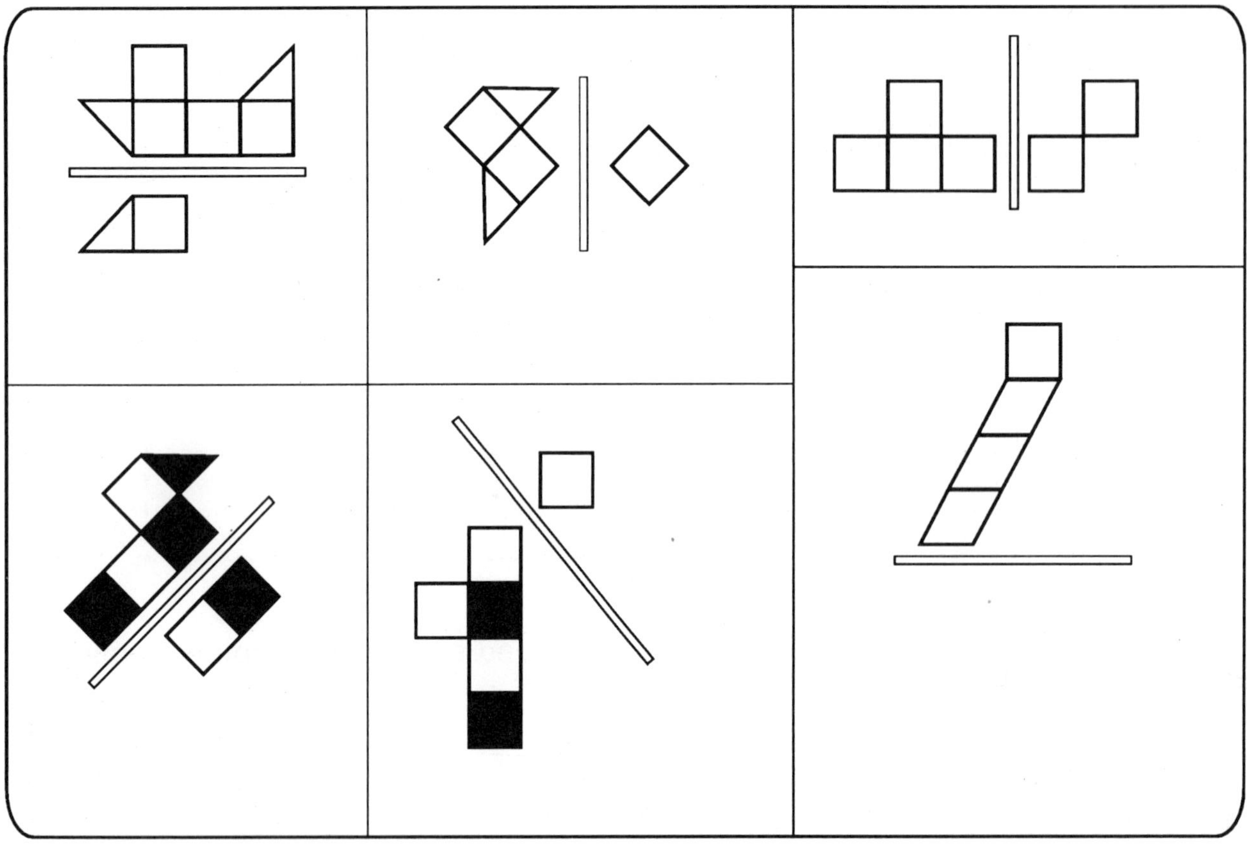

▲ Use a mirror on the shape below to make the shapes on the right .

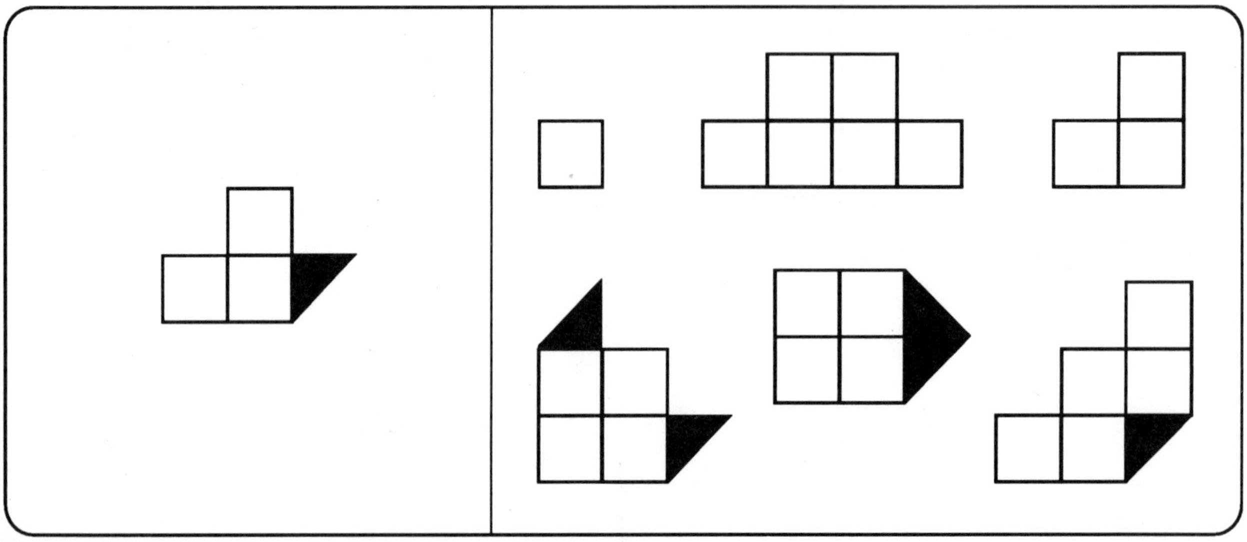

▲ Make up two of your own for someone to solve.
Draw them on the back of this sheet.

SHAPE, SPACE
AND MEASURES

Strip patterns, see page 40

Strip patterns

Name _____   Date _____

In Africa people make patterned strips by reflecting and sliding shapes.

This strip has been made by reflecting the triangle in a vertical axis of symmetry and then sliding it along a little and doing this over and over again. It could be made by flipping a triangle over.

▲ Explain how this strip was made. Use your own triangle to help.

▲ How were these strips made by reflecting and sliding triangles?

▲ Make up some of your own strip patterns using your triangles. You can slide them and reflect them horizontally or vertically. How many different strip patterns can you make?

SHAPE, SPACE
AND MEASURES

Four in a line, see page 42

Four in a line

Name(s) _____   Date _____

30°	**90°**	**190°**	**320°**
215°	**120°**	**20°**	**305°**
165°	**240°**	**295°**	**45°**
340°	**60°**	**265°**	**130°**

▲ Take it in turns to choose an angle from the game board.

▲ Use your card strips. Turn one of the arms so that you make an angle as close to the one that you have chosen. Keep it flat on the table while you work.

▲ Ask your partner to check your angle.

You 'win' the square if your angle is within 10° of the one you chose to make. The first player to make a line of 4 counters is the winner.

The line can be:

vertical   horizontal   diagonal

SHAPE, SPACE AND MEASURES

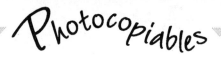
Rods

Name _____ Date _____

▲ Measure the length of each of your rods. Record them.
Remember! We write centimetres as cm

1▼

Colour of rod	Length of rod in cm

2▼

▲ Put the white rod and the red rod together, end to end.
What do they measure?

_____

▲ Use white, red, green, pink and yellow rods.
▲ Choose two and put them together, end to end.
What do they measure?

_____

▲ Do this again using a different combination of rods.
▲ Record your results on the chart.

3▼

Rods	Total length in cm
_____ and _____	
_____ and _____	
_____ and _____	
_____ and _____	
_____ and _____	
_____ and _____	
_____ and _____	
_____ and _____	
_____ and _____	

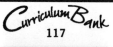
SHAPE, SPACE
AND MEASURES

Make a metre, see page 47

Make a metre

Name(s) _____ Date _____

▲ Use a sheet of paper to make a strip that is 1 metre long.
▲ Write about how you solved the problem.
What was hard? What was easy? What did you do when you got stuck?

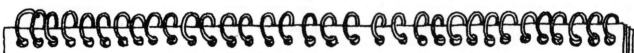

SHAPE, SPACE AND MEASURES

Pattern block perimeters, see page 49

Pattern block perimeters

Name _____ Date _____

You will need a
yellow hexagon,
a blue rhombus,
a green triangle
and a red
trapezium.

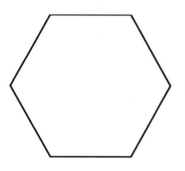

▲ Make this shape and
find its perimeter.
Estimate first.

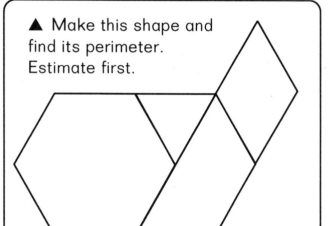

▲ Use the same blocks to
make different shapes.
Make surethat the blocks
join along edges.

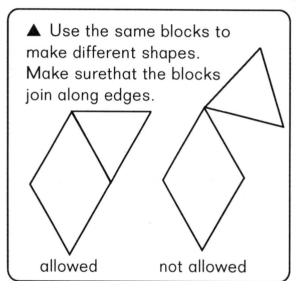

allowed   not allowed

▲ Use the blocks to make the shape with the longest perimeter.
▲ Use the blocks to make the shape with the shortest perimeter.
▲ Draw them and record their perimeters.

▲ Use the blocks to make a shape with a perimeter of 25cm.

**SHAPE, SPACE
AND MEASURES**

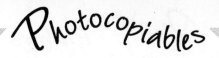

Small objects

Name _____ Date _____

You will need a matchbox.

▲ Find eight different objects that will fit into your matchbox. At least two of them should be less than 1cm long.

▲ Estimate and then measure them. Record your estimates and their lengths in this table.

object	my estimate of its length	length in mm	length in cm

Remember: 1mm equals 0.1cm, so the length of an item that measures 15mm can also be written as 1.5cm (1 centimetre and 5 tenths of a centimetre).

▲ Line up some of your objects and fit them into this space. Draw them.

What is their total length? _____mm or_____cm

▲ Find the three objects whose total length is closest to 3cm.

What is their total length? _____mm or _____cm

▲ Find the three objects whose total length is closest to 2cm.

What is their total length? _____mm or _____cm

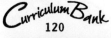

SHAPE, SPACE AND MEASURES

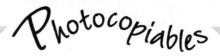
Measure me

Name _____   Date _____

People used to measure length using yards, feet and inches.
▲ Find out how these measures compare with the metric units that we use today and fill in the spaces to help you remember.

> 1 yard = cm   1 foot = cm   1 inch = cm

▲ Use the words *longer than* or *shorter than* to complete these sentences.

A yard is _____ a metre

A foot is _____ a metre and _____ a centimetre

An inch is _____ a metre and _____ a centimetre

▲ Label this picture to show some of your measurements in Imperial units and metric units.

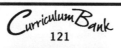

Rectangular areas (1)

Name _____ Date _____

This rectangle has an area of 12cm².

▲ Draw some more rectangles with an area of 12cm². Make sure that you label them.

▲ How many different rectangles can you draw with an area of 16cm²?

▲ How many different rectangles can you draw with an area of 8cm²?

▲ Choose an area. Can you make a rectangle with that area? Can you make more than one?

SHAPE, SPACE AND MEASURES

Rectangular areas, see page 56

Dotty grid

Name(s) _____   Date _____

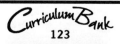
SHAPE, SPACE
AND MEASURES

Splodges, see page 58

Splodges

Name _____ Date _____

▲ Find the approximate area of these splodges and write them down.
Sometimes part of a square has been splodged. If more than half the square is covered then count it. If less than half a square has been covered do not count it.

▲ Use colouring pencils to make splodges on the back of this sheet.
▲ Use an acetate grid to help you find their approximate areas.

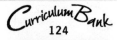

**SHAPE, SPACE
AND MEASURES**

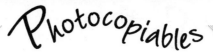
Slicing shapes

Name _____ Date _____

▲ Estimate the area of these shapes and write them down.
▲ Copy each shape or cut it out. Dissect each one and rearrange the pieces to make a rectangle.
▲ Find the area of each rectangle.

Parallelograms

Trapeziums

**SHAPE, SPACE
AND MEASURES**

Order the objects, see page 64

Order the objects

Name _____   Date _____

▲ Estimate the order of the objects.

object	estimate in grams	actual mass in grams

▲ Write the correct order.

SHAPE, SPACE
AND MEASURES

Potatoes, see page 66

Potatoes

Name(s) _____   Date _____

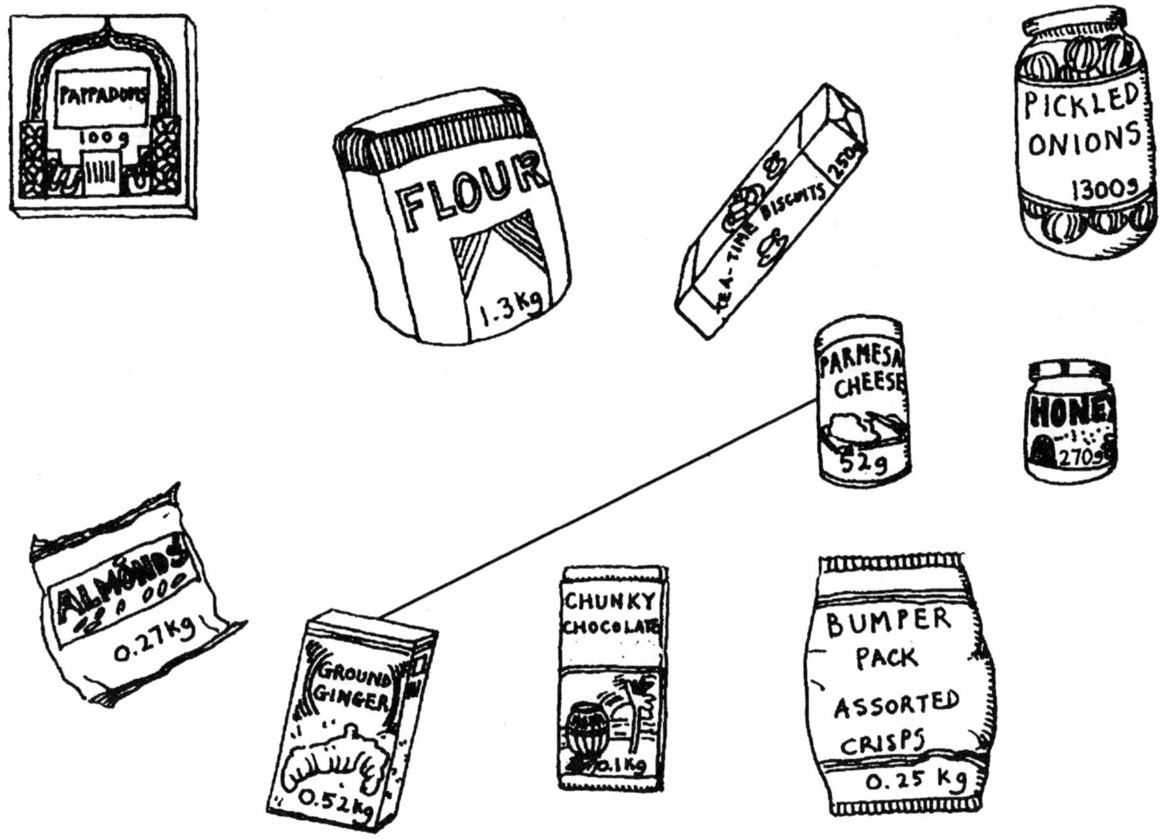

PAPPADUMS 100g

FLOUR 1.3kg

TEA-TIME BISCUITS 250g

PICKLED ONIONS 1300g

PARMESAN CHEESE 52g

HONEY 270g

ALMONDS 0.27kg

GROUND GINGER 0.52kg

CHUNKY CHOCOLATE 0.1kg

BUMPER PACK ASSORTED CRISPS 0.25 kg

▲ Each of these labels belongs with another. Join them up. One has been done for you.

▲ Take three potatoes. Estimate their total mass. Check your estimate on the scales. Record their mass as grams and then as kilograms.

	estimate of total mass	actual mass in grams	actual mass in kilograms
1st go			
2nd go			
3rd go			

▲ Write the total mass of all your potatoes in grams and then in kilograms.

_____ g   _____ kg

SHAPE, SPACE AND MEASURES

Good buys

Name(s) _____   Date _____

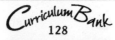

▲ Compare the food by answering these questions. Explain how you got your answers.

Which weighs more, two pieces of fruit or the box of cereal? What is the difference in weight?

_____

_____

If eight people emptied the cereal packet by having a bowl each, what would the weight of each portion be?

_____

_____

How much does the cereal *box* weigh?

_____

_____

▲ Compare the weight of a biscuit from each of the packets.
Which of the packets of biscuits gives better value for money?

_____

_____

SHAPE, SPACE AND MEASURES

Photocopiables

Mystery containers, see page 74

Mystery containers

Name(s) _____ Date _____

▲ Draw each Mystery container in the space provided.
▲ Write how much you estimated it would hold.
▲ Write how much it actually held when you measured.

| Mystery Container A | Estimate |
| | Actual |

| Mystery Container B | Estimate |
| | Actual |

| Mystery Container C | Estimate |
| | Actual |

| Mystery Container D | Estimate |
| | Actual |

| Mystery Container E | Estimate |
| | Actual |

How much does it hold?

Name(s) _____ Date _____

Work in pairs.

▲ Take 5 containers from the capacity table and a litre measuring jug.

▲ Make an estimate of the capacity of the first container and record it in the second column of the table.

▲ Fill it with sand or water and use the measuring jug to find out how much it actually holds. Record your result in the third column.

▲ Do the same for all the containers.

container	estimate	capacity when measured
A		
B		
C		
D		
E		

▲ For which container did you make the best estimate?

▲ For which container did you make the worst estimate?

▲ Why did you find it hard to make a good estimate of this container?

SHAPE, SPACE AND MEASURES

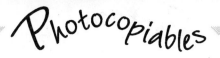

Find the volume, see page 77

Find the volume (1)

Name _____ Date _____

▲ Build three different cubes. Each time you build one draw it. Show how you worked out its volume.

Cubes

▲ Now build three different cuboids. Draw each one and show how you calculated its volume.

Cuboids

SHAPE, SPACE
AND MEASURES

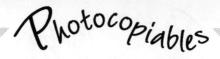

Find the volume, see page 77

Find the volume (2)

Name _____   Date _____

Ben built this model. He found its volume by counting the number of layers and the number of cubes in each layer.

number of layers	number of cubes in a layer	volume of model
2	6	12

▲ Make some more cuboids. Use the chart like Ben did to help you find the volume of each one.

number of layers	number of cubes in a layer	volume of model

SHAPE, SPACE
AND MEASURES

Pints and litres, see page 79

Pints and litres

Name _____   Date _____

A litre is more than a pint. How much more? _____

When 1 pint of liquid is poured into a litre container, how many millilitres does it measure?

▲ Draw the water level on the picture below to show what happened when you poured 1 pint of water into a container which measured in millilitres.

—1000ml
— 950ml
—900ml
— 850ml
—800ml
— 750ml
—700ml
— 650 ml
—600ml
— 550ml
— 500ml
— 450ml
—400ml
— 350ml
—300ml
— 250ml
—200ml
— 150ml
— 100ml
— 50ml

▲ Complete these sentences.

1 pint is equivalent to _____ ml

2 pints are equivalent to _____ l

1 pint is about a third / a half / a quarter of a litre

(put a circle round the correct answer).

1 litre is about three / a half / one and three quarter pints

(put a circle round the correct answer).

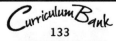

SHAPE, SPACE
AND MEASURES

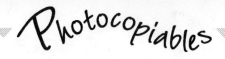

What's the time?

Name _____   Date _____

▲ Choose six TV programmes and find out what time
they start. Record them on this table.

	name of programme	starting time
1		
2		
3		
4		
5		
6		

Programme Name

7.35 or twenty five
_____

minutes to eight
_____

▲ Show the time on the clocks then write the times underneath.

Programme 1

_____
_____

Programme 2

_____
_____

Programme 3

_____
_____

Programme 4

_____
_____

Programme 5

_____
_____

Programme 6

_____
_____

**SHAPE, SPACE
AND MEASURES**

My TV week

Name _____ Date _____

What are your TV watching habits?
How much time do you spend watching soap operas in a typical week?
▲ Use this space to work out and record your answer.

How much time do you spend watching comedy programmes in a typical week?
▲ Use this space to work out and record your answer.

How much time do you spend watching music programmes in a typical week?
▲ Use this space to work out and record your answer.

How much time do you spend watching sport in a typical week?
▲ Use this space to work out and record your answer.

How much time do you spend watching TV in a typical week?
▲ Use this space to work out and record your answer.

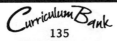

SHAPE, SPACE AND MEASURES

Three-dimensional shape, see page 90

Aspect of assessment	PoS	Evidence and outcomes	Name and date	Comments	Name and date	Comments
Describing shapes.	2a	Did the child: ...describe the shapes accurately?				
Using geometrical language.	2a	... use the relevant mathematical terminology to describe shapes?				
Making three-dimensional shapes.	2b	... make their own model of a three-dimensional shape?				
Recognising congruence.	2c	... use a prepared net?				
Recognising congruence.	2c	... use a construction kit?				
Recognising congruence.	2c	... use ruler and pencil to draw the net when constructing their shape?				
Recognising congruence.	2c	... identify congruent faces?				

SHAPE, SPACE
AND MEASURES

Photocopiables

1

▲   Write about three-dimensional shapes and their properties. Use drawings if they help you to explain.

▲ Think about the shape and number of faces, the number of edges and vertices, symmetry.

Cubes, cuboids and prisms

Pyramids, tetrahedra and cones

Spheres and cylinders

SHAPE, SPACE AND MEASURES

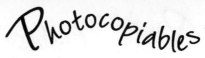
Three-dimensional shape, see page 90

1

Net of a cube

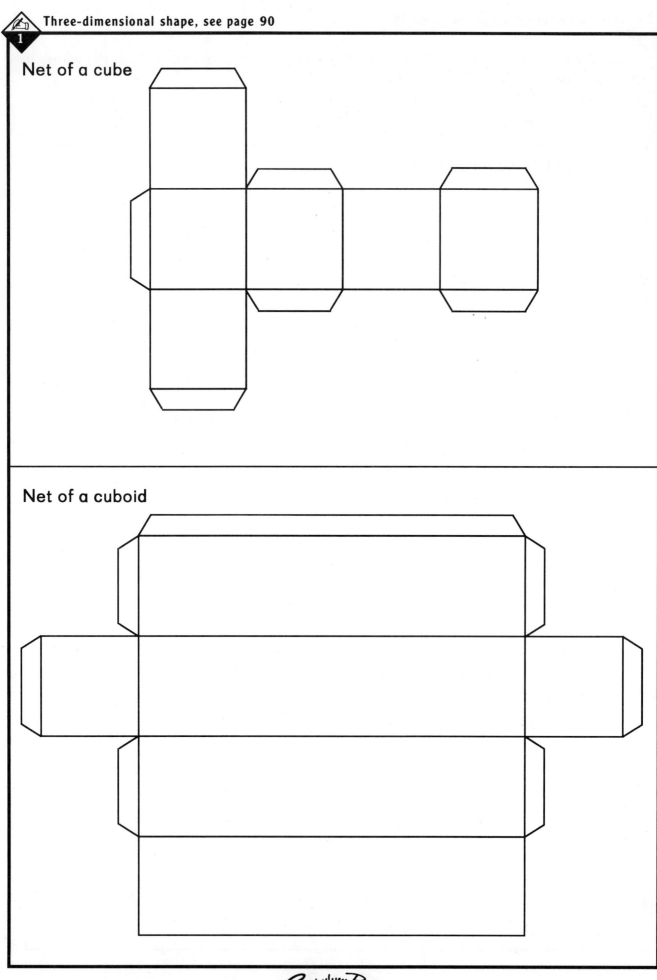

Net of a cuboid

SHAPE, SPACE
AND MEASURES

Three-dimensional shape, see page 90

1

Net of a regular tetrahedron
(triangular-based pyramid)

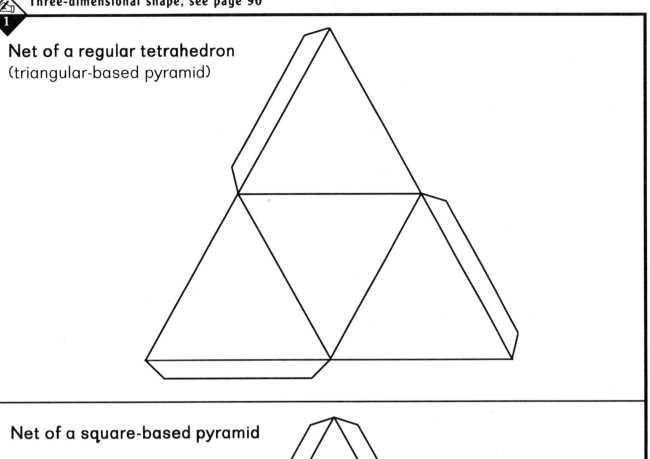

Net of a square-based pyramid

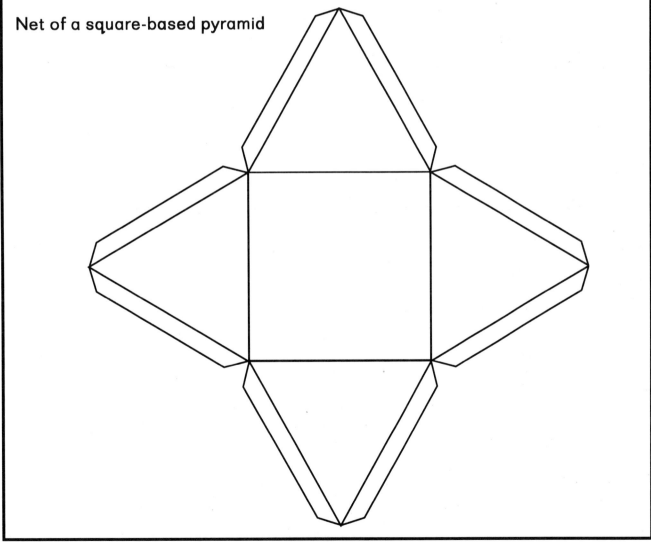

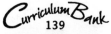

SHAPE, SPACE
AND MEASURES

Net of a
triangular
prism

Net of a cylinder

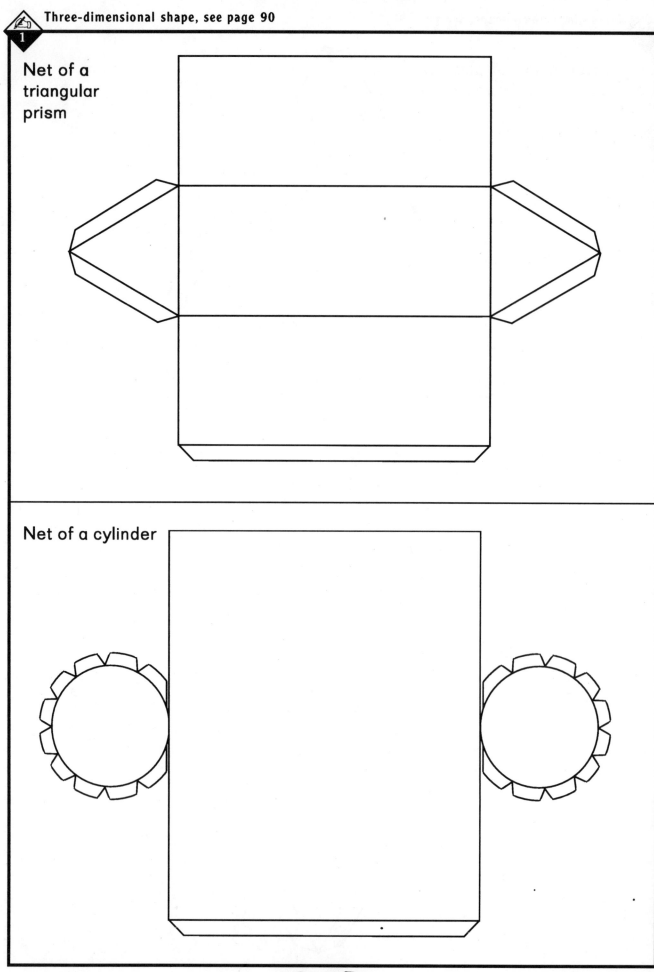

Two-dimensional shape, see page 91

Aspect of assessment	PoS	Evidence and outcomes	Name and date	Comments	Name and date	Comments
Using mathematical language to describe properties.	2a	Did the child: ...use precise mathematical language to describe the features of the shapes?				
Classifying shapes.	2b	... classify the shapes according to a rule?				
Recognising reflective symmetries.	2c	... find another way to classify the set of shapes?				
Recognising rotational symmetries.	2c	... classify the shapes according to the number of axes of symmetry?				
Understanding congruence.	2c	... identify the rotational symmetries of a shape?				
Making shapes.	2c	...draw shapes with different orientations on grid paper?				

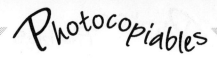

Two-dimensional shape, see page 91

▲ Sort your set of shapes into those that have at least three axes of symmetry and those that do not. Write or draw the shapes on the chart.

Shapes with at least 3 axes of symmetry	Shapes with less than 3 axes of symmetry

Mystery shape

I have 4 sides of equal length. I have 4 equal angles. I have 4 axes of symmetry. I have rotational symmetry of order 4. What am I?

▲ Make up your own clues for a mystery shape.

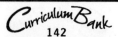

SHAPE, SPACE AND MEASURES

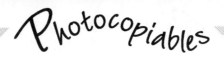

▲ Look at these triangles. Colour the 3 triangles which would fit on top of each other if you cut them out.

▲ Use the grid paper. Draw 3 rectangles that would fit on top of each other if you cut them out. Make them point in different directions if you can.

SHAPE, SPACE AND MEASURES

Aspect of assessment	PoS	Evidence and outcomes	Name and date	Comments	Name and date	Comments
Transforming two-dimensional shapes by translation.	3a	Did the child: ... make a pattern using sliding movement?				
Transforming two-dimensional shapes by rotation.	3a	... continue the pattern by rotating the shape?				
Transforming two-dimensional shapes by reflection.	3a	... reflect the pattern in the mirror line?				
Measuring rotation.	3c	... identify that the shape had been rotated by 90 degrees or a right angle or a quarter turn?				

Dan coloured 5 squares to make a shape:

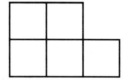

▲ Use Dan's shape to make a repeating pattern.
▲ Draw the first line of your pattern above the mirror line. Draw its reflection in the mirror below.

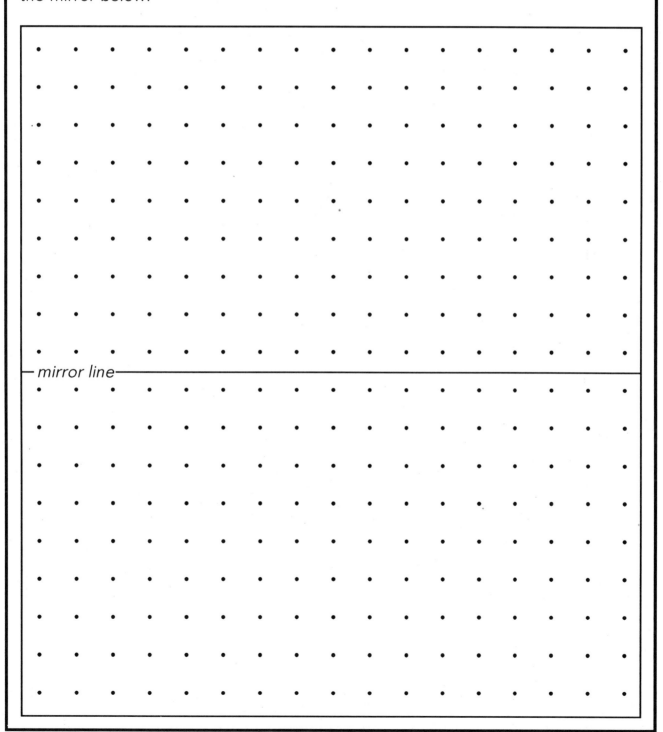

mirror line

SHAPE, SPACE AND MEASURES

Photocopiables

▲ **Position and movement, see page 93**

3

Dan made another
shape. He made a new pattern:

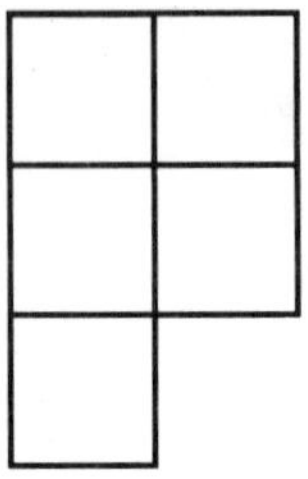

He turned his shape:

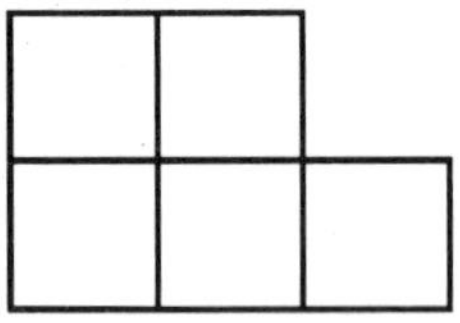

He turned it again the same way:

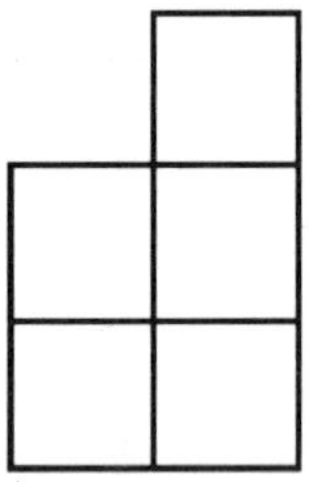

▲ Show how Dan's shape looked after he had turned it again the same way:

▲ How much did Dan turn his shape each time? _____

**SHAPE, SPACE
AND MEASURES**

4

Aspect of assessment	PoS	Evidence and outcomes	Name and date	Comments	Name and date	Comments
Making estimates using standard units of length.	4a	Did the child: ... make sensible estimates of the length of the parcels' edges?				
Making estimates using standard units of mass.	4a	... make sensible estimates of the mass of the parcels?				
Using standard units of length.	4a	... suggest appropriate standard units for measuring length? ... measure accurately using cm and mm?				
Converting between metric units of length and mass.	4a	Was the child: ... able to convert between cm and mm? ... able to convert between kg and g?				

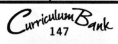

4

Length, area and mass, see page 94

Aspect of assessment	PoS	Evidence and outcomes	Name and date	Comments	Name and date	Comments
Using standard units of mass.	4a	Did the child: ... suggest appropriate standard units for measuring mass?				
Using measuring instruments.	4a	... measure accurately using kg and g? ... use scales, rulers and area grids correctly?				
Finding areas.	4c	... use strategies based on counting to find areas? ... use the formula $a = l \times b$?				
Finding perimeters.	4c	... find perimeters of faces?				

Length, area and mass, see page 94

▲ Use this chart to show what you found out about the length, area, mass and perimeter of the parcels. Try to present your results clearly so that the reader can understand them easily.

SHAPE, SPACE AND MEASURES

Capacity and volume, see page 96

5

Aspect of assessment	PoS	Evidence and outcomes	Name and date	Comments
Making estimates with standard units of capacity.	4a	Did the child: ...make sensible estimates?		
Choosing and using appropriate measuring instruments.	4a	... choose and use the correct measuring instruments?		
Reading scales.	4b	... read the scale on the measuring jug accurately? ... read it to the nearest labelled division?		
Understanding the relationship between units of capacity.	4a	... convert between metric units of capacity?		
Finding volumes by counting methods.	4c	... use strategies based on counting to find volume? ... calculate using the number of cubes in a layer and the number of layers?		

SHAPE, SPACE
AND MEASURES

5

▲ Put your set of containers in order of estimated capacity.
▲ Draw each one and record your estimates of their capacity.

▲ Now find a way to check your estimates.
Is the order different?
▲ Draw the set in order of capacity and write how much each container held.

▲ Choose two containers.
If you filled them both up with sand and then put both lots into one big container how much sand would there be altogether?

_____

▲ Write your answer a different way.

_____

Sarah's two containers contained 1300ml of sand.
▲ Write this in litres and millilitres.

_____litres _____millilitres

Samir's two containers held 500ml of sand.
▲ Write this in litres.

_____

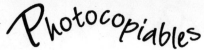

5

▲ One of these nets will fold up to make a cuboid with a volume of 36cm³.

▲ Use centimetre cubes to help you find out which one it is.

What is the volume of the other cuboids?

SHAPE, SPACE
AND MEASURES

Time, see page 97

6

Aspect of assessment	PoS	Evidence and outcomes	Name and date	Comments	Name and date	Comments
Recording times.	4a	Did the child: … record the time to the nearest minute on an analogue clock-face?				
Converting between the 12- and 24-hour clock.	4b	… translate between 12-hour and 24-hour times?				
Using timing instruments.	4b	… use the stopwatch correctly? … read times to the nearest second? … read times to the nearest tenth of a second?				

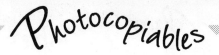

Time, see page 97

6

▲ Show the times that your teacher tells you on the clock-faces below.

▲ Show the 24-hour clock times that your teacher tells you as 12-hour times on the clock-faces below.

SHAPE, SPACE
AND MEASURES

USING AND APPLYING MATHEMATICS

This section of the Programme of Study should be set in the context of the other sections. It is very important that the children are given opportunities to use and apply mathematics in practical activities, in real-life problems and within mathematics itself. Using and applying mathematics can only occur in relation to the knowledge and understanding of other aspects of the curriculum. It is an approach and not a body of knowledge in itself. Children should be given the opportunity to explain their thinking to support the development of their reasoning. Aspects of the using and applying approach are included within almost all of the activities in this book. The table on pages 156 and 157 shows where there may be opportunities for the teacher to incorporate using and applying mathematics into activities.

The Programme of Study for using and applying mathematics is divided into three main sub-sections: making and monitoring decisions to solve problems; developing mathematical language and forms of communication; and developing mathematical reasoning. Each sub-section is divided into three or four separate aspects.

The 'using and applying' aspects of the mathematics National Curriculum provide the context within which the content of the curriculum is taught and learned. There has to be a balance between those activities which develop knowledge skills and understanding, and those which develop the ability to tackle practical problems. The processes involved in the 'using and applying' dimension enable pupils to make use of and communicate their mathematical knowledge; for many pupils this is the main point in learning mathematics.

The diagram below shows the context, content and process dimensions of mathematics teaching.

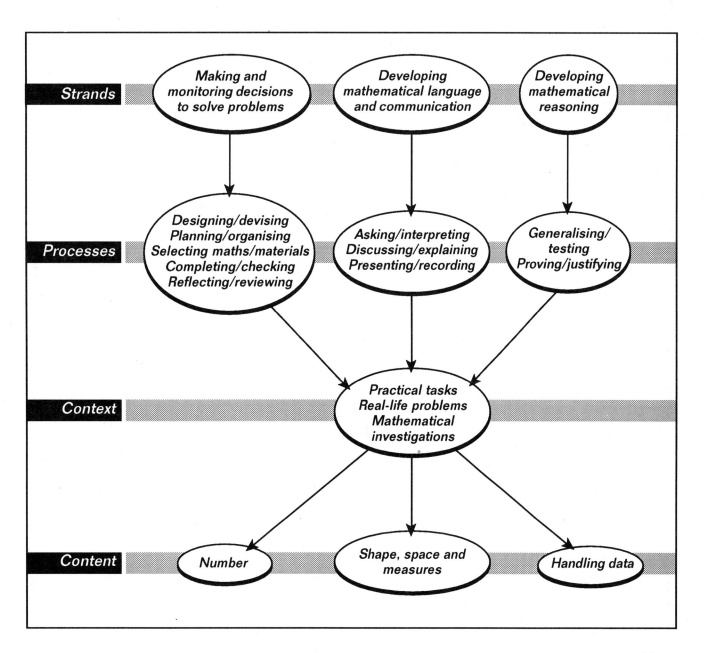

Strands
- Making and monitoring decisions to solve problems
- Developing mathematical language and communication
- Developing mathematical reasoning

Processes
- Designing/devising Planning/organising Selecting maths/materials Completing/checking Reflecting/reviewing
- Asking/interpreting Discussing/explaining Presenting/recording
- Generalising/ testing Proving/justifying

Context
- Practical tasks Real-life problems Mathematical investigations

Content
- Number
- Shape, space and measures
- Handling data

SHAPE, SPACE AND MEASURES

		SOLVING PROBLEMS				COMMUNICATION			LOGICAL REASONING			
	ACTIVITIES	Pupils select and use the appropriate mathematics and materials.	Pupils try different mathematical approaches; identify and obtain information needed to carry out their work.	Pupils develop their own mathematical strategies and look for ways to overcome difficulties.	Pupils check their results and consider whether they are reasonable.	Pupils understand and use the language of number, properties and movements of shapes...	Pupils use diagrams, graphs and simple algebraic symbols.	Pupils present information and results clearly, and explain the reasons for their choice of presentation.	Pupils understand and investigate general statements.	Pupils search for pattern in their results.	Pupils make general statements of their own, based on evidence they have produced.	Pupils explain their reasoning.
		a	b	c	d	a	b	c	a	b	c	d
Three-dimensional shape	Memory game					●					●	●
	Cubes	●	●	●		●	●		●		●	●
	Prisms	●	●	●		●	●		●		●	●
	Sorting three-dimensional shapes	●	●		●	●	●		●	●	●	
	Symmetries of three-dimensional shapes	●	●	●	●	●			●		●	●
	Spots and nets	●	●	●	●	●					●	●
Two-dimensional shape	Fold and count		●			●	●	●			●	●
	Two cuts		●	●		●		●		●	●	●
	Find the shape					●						
	Triangles		●	●	●				●		●	●
	Quadrilaterals			●		●				●	●	●
	Turning and shrinking shapes	●	●	●		●		●	●			●
Position and movement	Tile patterns	●	●			●						
	Pieces	●			●	●		●				
	Shapes and mirrors	●	●	●	●	●	●			●		●
	Strip patterns	●	●	●		●						
	Four in a line	●			●	●						
	Co-ordinated shapes	●	●	●	●	●	●	●		●	●	●
Length	Rods	●	●			●						
	Make a metre	●		●	●	●						
	Pattern block perimeters		●	●	●	●		●			●	●
	Small objects				●	●				●		
	Measure me	●		●	●	●	●					

Using & applying

	ACTIVITIES	SOLVING PROBLEMS				COMMUNICATION			LOGICAL REASONING			
		Pupils select and use the appropriate mathematics and materials.	Pupils try different mathematical approaches; identify and obtain information needed to carry out their work.	Pupils develop their own mathematical strategies and look for ways to overcome difficulties.	Pupils check their results and consider whether they are reasonable.	Pupils understand and use the language of number, properties and movements of shapes...	Pupils use diagrams, graphs and simple algebraic symbols.	Pupils present information and results clearly, and explain the reasons for their choice of presentation.	Pupils understand and investigate general statements.	Pupils search for pattern in their results.	Pupils make general statements of their own, based on evidence they have produced.	Pupils explain their reasoning.
		a	b	c	d	a	b	c	a	b	c	d
Area	Rectangular areas	▓	▓			▓		▓	▓		▓	
	Splodges			▓	▓	▓					▓	▓
	Outsides and insides	▓	▓	▓	▓	▓		▓	▓		▓	
	Slicing shapes	▓						▓				
Mass	Order the objects	▓	▓	▓	▓	▓		▓				▓
	Potatoes	▓	▓		▓	▓					▓	▓
	Good buys	▓	▓	▓		▓					▓	▓
	Metric and Imperial units of mass			▓	▓	▓			▓			▓
Capacity and volume	Mystery containers			▓	▓	▓		▓		▓	▓	▓
	How much does it hold?	▓	▓	▓	▓	▓						
	Find the volume	▓	▓	▓	▓	▓	▓	▓			▓	▓
	Pints and litres	▓	▓			▓		▓	▓			▓
Time	What's the time?			▓		▓	▓					
	How long does it take?			▓	▓						▓	▓
	My TV week	▓	▓	▓	▓	▓		▓				
	24-hour time line					▓	▓					
Assessment	Three-dimensional shape	▓	▓	▓	▓	▓	▓	▓	▓		▓	▓
	Two-dimensional shape	▓	▓	▓		▓			▓			
	Position and movement	▓	▓		▓	▓	▓					
	Length, mass and area	▓	▓	▓	▓	▓	▓	▓			▓	▓
	Capacity and volume	▓	▓	▓	▓	▓		▓				▓
	Time	▓			▓	▓	▓					

INFORMATION TECHNOLOGY WITHIN SPACE, SHAPE AND MEASURES AT KS2

Main IT focus
Although the work in this area of mathematics can give rise to work across a range of different IT applications this section looks more closely at two which are particularly relevant for this work.

Drawing software
This type of software is particularly useful in the exploration of shape and space as it allows children to create and manipulate geometrical shapes and patterns.

These packages have a range of features to aid the drawing of regular shapes. The first is the ability to have a background grid which can be set to specific units; this assists the drawing of lines of specific lengths or for use in scale drawings. There will also be an option to 'snap to grid' which ensures that when a child draws a line which may not exactly reach the grid dot it will automatically join up to it. This is useful for drawing regular shapes and for making sure lines are vertical or horizontal.

Features to allow specific shapes such as rectangles and circles to be drawn as well as freehand lines and irregular closed shapes are available. Some packages also have the facility to 'undo' so that mistakes can be corrected without rubbing out the whole picture. Once children have mastered the initial drawing techniques they should be shown how to copy shapes, either by cutting or deleting them from the drawing and then pasting them back.

Where the investigation of pattern is important the teacher can set up the background grid in advance and create a toolbox of useful shapes which can be set along the bottom of the drawing screen. This initial screen and toolbox can be saved as a file so that all the shapes needed are immediately available for the child to use.

The ability to draw a range of geometric shapes makes the drawing package an ideal tool for exploring areas such as tessellations, designing nets and exploring the properties of shapes. However, children will also need to be shown how to rotate and flip objects so that they can be fitted together in different ways. By using these facilities it is easy to make complex pictures from several different shapes called 'objects' which are 'grouped' to make a single object. The net for a cube can be made from six squares, each drawn individually but grouped to form a single object which can be copied, rotated, moved or re-scaled in a few moves.

Using LOGO
LOGO is a powerful programming language which was specifically written for education. Although it is possible to write complex programs using LOGO most children will know

it from using one subset of the language called *Turtle Graphics*. One of the important issues in using LOGO is that children are in control of their learning; they decide how to tackle a problem, and there can be many different 'correct' solutions to the same problem depending on the experience of the child.

Children's first use of LOGO is often through the use of a floor robot such as ROAMER or a floor turtle controlled from the computer. The next step is to use the computer screen as the drawing area rather than the floor. Children will start in 'Command' mode where, as they type a command, its effects are immediately seen on the screen.

To draw a square in command mode, for example, they would type:

    FD 100
    RT 90
    FD 100
    RT 90
    FD 100
    RT 90
    FD 100
    RT 90

For more complex shapes this can become a long process and children will want to find shorter ways of achieving the same results. This is the time to introduce the REPEAT command which can reduce drawing a square to:

    REPEAT 4 [FD100 RT90]
    END

The next step is to define a new procedure (known as a primitive) which uses this REPEAT, for example

    TO SQUARE
    REPEAT 4 [FD100 RT90]
    END

Another stage forward would be to include variables so that squares with different lengths can be drawn from a single command such as SQUARE 250 (as described on page 33).

When using Screen Turtle in the classroom children need time, initially to explore and experiment, but also to develop and practise the skills and new commands as they acquire them. Although children will usually work in pairs or small groups, so that they can support each other, share ideas and discuss their work, it is vital there are good levels of teacher intervention and interaction to ensure that new ideas can be introduced at appropriate points. As a teacher there is a great temptation to introduce new commands such as REPEAT too early or without sufficient explanation and examples. The skill of the teacher is in knowing when children are ready to move on.

If you are using LOGO with the children you will need to spend time with the software yourself so that you are aware of dialect of LOGO language your software uses, the difficulties of, for example, drawing a pentagon or a circle, what commands are available and how to write repeats and create procedures.

IT links

Mathematics provides teachers with abundant opportunities to develop children's IT capability through communicating and handling information and modelling. It can also be used to develop children's mathematical understanding through the use of specific software. New software related to National Curriculum Mathematics appears regularly and it has been possible to mention only a few of the more relevant and useful titles within the activities. However teachers may want to supplement the activities with other software as it becomes available.

AREA OF IT	SOFTWARE	ACTIVITIES (PAGE NOS.)							
		CHAP 1	CHAP 2	CHAP 3	CHAP 4	CHAP 5	CHAP 6	CHAP 7	CHAP 8
Communicating Info	Word processor						66		82
Communicating Info	Art			39					
Communicating Info	Drawing	15,17,21	27,30	36,39		56			
Communicating Info	Framework software			36					
Information handling	Database								85
Information handling	Branching database	19							
Information handling	Graphing software						70	77,79	85
Modelling	Spreadsheet				49,53		68,70	77,79	
Control/Modelling	LOGO		30,31,33	41					
Control	Control box								84
Control	ROAMER/PIPP			41,42					
Monitoring									84

SOFTWARE TYPE	BBC/MASTER	RISCOS	NIMBUS/186	WINDOWS	MACINTOSH
Word processor	Pendown Folio	Pendown Desk Top Folio	All Write Write On	Word for Windows Kid Works 2 Creative Writer	Kid Works 2 Easy Works Creative Writer
Framework		My World 2		My World 2	
Art package		Kid Pix Splash	PaintSpa Splat	Colour Magic Kid Pix 2	Kid Pix 2
Drawing		Draw Vector		Claris Works Oak Draw	Claris Works
Database	Grass	Junior Pinpoint KeyNote	Grass Sparks	Sparks Claris Works	Claris Works Easy Works
Branching database	Branch	ReTreeval Tree	Branch	Tree	
Graphing software	Data Show	GraphIT Data plot	Datagraph	Datagraph Easy Works	Easy Works
LOGO	Dart LOGO	First Logo Win Logo		First Logo Win Logo Micro Worlds Project Builder	Logo Write Micro Worlds Project Builder
Spreadsheet	Grasshopper Pigeonhole	Grasshopper Advantage Key Count	Grasshopper	Excel Starting Grid Claris Works Sparks	Claris Works
Measurement	Sense-it	Junior Insight	Investigate	Insight Investigate	Insight

159

SHAPE, SPACE
AND MEASURES

	ENGLISH	SCIENCE	HISTORY	GEOGRAPHY	D & T	ART	MUSIC	PE
THREE-DIMENSIONAL SHAPE	Describing and talking about shapes using the correct mathematical terminology. Giving and following instructions for constructing three-dimensional shapes.	Exploring shapes as part of physical properties of materials.	Examining the shapes used in building of different periods.	Describing features of localities. Representing three-dimensional features in two dimensions on maps and plans.	Methods of reinforcing loaded structures.	Using three-dimensional shapes to visualise and make patterns. Presenting work in three dimensions.		Forming shapes with partners and in small groups. Exploring space in apparatus work.
TWO-DIMENSIONAL SHAPE	Describing and talking about shapes using the correct mathematical terminology. Giving and following instructions for constructing two-dimensional shapes.	Consideration of the way forces can distort the shape of objects.	Examining the ways in which the Victorians used shape in creating tiles.	Making maps and plans.	Triangles as strong shapes in constructing models and buildings.	Experimenting with tools and techniques to create patterns in two dimensions.	Using shape as part of graphical notation in composition.	Appreciating the patterns made in dance forms from different times and places.
POSITION AND MOVEMENT	Describing routes, describing the orientation and positions of shapes. Giving instructions for making patterns.	Considering the way that forces acting on objects can cause a change of direction. Identifying changes of position of Earth, Moon and Sun.	Transforming simple shapes to produce Greek patterns.	Coordinates as four-figure grid references. Using angles in bearings and compass points and bearings.	Using simple mechanisms to facilitate movement.	Using translation, reflection and rotation to create patterns. Identifying how pattern, line and space are used in images.	Responding to music through movements.	Changes of shape, reflecting a sequence of movements in dance. Describing paths made by balls during games.
MEASURES	Comparing objects, events and distances using mathematical language.	Using standard measures appropriately during scientific enquiry.	The development of measures in other cultures and times e.g. Egyptian, Greek.	Estimating and measuring direction and distance. Scale and ratio in mapwork. Measuring changes in temperature, rainfall and sunshine.	Measuring, marking out and cutting when planning and making. Weighing ingredients in food technology.	Studying perspective. Estimating amount of materials needed.	Listening to and performing pieces using different time signatures. Length of notes – minims, semibreves etc.	Estimating and measuring stride length and distance of throws. Timing during athletics events.

SHAPE, SPACE AND MEASURES